The Three Marjories

The Three Marjories

Marjory Stoneman Douglas,
Marjorie Kinnan Rawlings,
Marjorie Harris Carr, and
Their Contributions to Florida

Sandra Wallus Sammons

Pineapple Press, Inc.
Sarasota, Florida

Pineapple Press
An imprint of The Rowman & Littlefield Publishing Group, Inc.
4501 Forbes Blvd., Ste. 200
Lanham, MD 20706
www.rowman.com

Distributed by NATIONAL BOOK NETWORK

British Library Cataloguing in Publication Information available

Library of Congress Cataloging-in-Publication Data available

ISBN 978-1-68334-035-5 (paperback)
ISBN 978-1-68334-036-2 (e-book)

Dedicated to my granddaughter, Aja Marie Sammons,
and Charley Ziesmer, Jackson Hoefer, and little
Ellie Jean Ziesmer, expected in July. Love to you all.

Contents

Foreword

In *The Three Marjories: Marjory Stoneman Douglas, Marjorie Kinnan Rawlings, Marjorie Harris Carr, and Their Contributions to Florida*, Sandra Wallus Sammons introduces young readers to three extraordinary women who fell in love with Florida and devoted their lives to saving it. In this important new book, Sammons's lyrical prose both educates and inspires. A seasoned author of multiple books in the Pineapple Young Reader Biographies series, Sammons weaves together the fascinating lives and work of Douglas, Rawlings, and Carr, revealing little-known connections between these Florida transplants, who each fought to preserve the natural beauty of Florida through their writing and activism.

Throughout this engaging book, young readers are encouraged to explore Florida and raise their voices to protect its fragile ecosystems for future generations, the way the three Marjories did in the twentieth century. At the time Marjory Stoneman Douglas and Marjorie

Harris Carr made Florida their home, women still did not have the right to vote. Nevertheless, they persisted, and—along with Pulitzer Prize–winning author Marjorie Kinnan Rawlings—they used the power of the pen, grassroots activism, or a combination of both to stand up for Florida's wild places and the unique plants and animals that live in the Sunshine State.

Marjorie Kinnan Rawlings's 1938 novel *The Yearling* and her 1942 book *Cross Creek* reveal the deep affinity she had with the wildlife and rugged landscape surrounding the tiny hamlet of Cross Creek in north-central Florida. Although there is no evidence that Rawlings and Marjorie Harris Carr ever met, they shared a love of the ancient, crooked river that runs through the Ocala National Forest: the Ocklawaha. Carr fought until her death to protect and restore the Ocklawaha River, which was dammed during construction of the ill-fated Cross Florida Barge Canal. Carr and the organization she cofounded to save the Ocklawaha River, Florida Defenders of the Environment (FDE), succeeded in stopping construction of the canal. Today, FDE is still working to restore the Ocklawaha and over twenty lost springs that are submerged under the dammed river's flooded waters.

In addition to the "Three Marjories," Sammons also introduces young readers to Marjorie Carr's husband, "The Man Who Saved Sea Turtles," as historian Frederick Rowe Davis titled his 2007 biography of Archie Carr. Archie's groundbreaking research in Honduras, Costa Rica, and Africa led to important protections for sea turtles and sea turtle nesting sites around the world.

Marjory Stoneman Douglas's writing and activism helped do for the Everglades what Archie Carr's research accomplished for sea turtles. In Douglas's 1947 book *The Everglades: River of Grass*, she helped readers gain a new appreciation for a beautiful part of Florida that had previously been viewed as a wasteland. And as Douglas's biographer, the Pulitzer Prize–winning historian Jack E. Davis, has noted, as she neared the end of her 108 years on this earth, Douglas said the "most important thing is to prepare competent people to follow you."

"We can all follow in the three Marjories' footsteps," Sammons writes.

This exciting new look at Florida's "Three Marjories" calls upon new generations of Floridians to join their voices together and become strong advocates for Florida's environment. Like Marjory Stoneman Douglas before her, Sandra Sammons stresses the important role young people play in protecting the earth. This well-researched book will appeal not only to young readers, but to all who are lucky enough to call Florida their home.

—Dr. Peggy Macdonald, author, *Marjorie Harris Carr:*
Defender of Florida's Environment

Acknowledgments

Thanks to all those researchers before me who have written so clearly and in-depth about the subjects I've wanted to write about. Their work made mine much easier.

Thanks to June Cussen at Pineapple Press for allowing me to do "just one more book."

Thanks to Helena Berg, my copyeditor, who has been a huge help with making my words flow.

Thanks to Dr. Peggy Macdonald, whose book *Marjorie Harris Carr: Defender of Florida's Environment*, was an enormous help in my research.

Thanks to Mimi Carr for reading over the book and sharing more stories, and for the use of photos of her family.

Thanks to Steve and Misty Sammons for sharing their photographs. They put on boots to walk through the "river of grass" to find the ghost orchid and trekked through many other wild places to find wild, natural Florida.

Thanks to those who read over the manuscript before publication: Mimi Carr, Dr. Peggy Macdonald, Phyllis Lewis, Bob Sammons, Steve and Misty Sammons, and Aja Sammons.

Thanks to so many who supported me during my writing time: Dave Sammons, Kris Huddleston, Calvin Sammons, Tawny and Brady Gutierrez, Donna Zimmerman, Aviva Kahn, Lorie Newman, Karen and Dave Brzezowski, Jody and Tom Sanders, and Jo Anne Sikes.

Introduction

The explorers who were brave enough to cross the Atlantic Ocean five hundred years ago named the land "La Florida" with good reason. It was springtime, the season of "Pascua Florida," or "feast of flowers," and there were many flowers and many different shades of green on the trees! Would this place also have gold? Even without gold, this land they encountered was definitely worth exploring.

What they found were deep woods and wide savannas, and native tribes who had lived there for thousands of years. The natives lived in harmony with their natural surroundings, eating fish from the clean rivers and animals that made their homes in the thick forests. They survived well on the bounty of the land around them.

There were many trees, but the natives only took what they needed for their shelter or canoes. Huge stands of virgin cypress were still there when later explorers, including John and William Bartram in the 1700s, were

Ghost orchid. Photo by Misty Sammons.

walking through Florida. There were spreading oaks that were so awesome that William Bartram could scarcely believe his eyes. The earliest explorers also found the woods full of animals. William Bartram, later writing about the alligators he saw, said that there were so many in one river he crossed that he almost could have walked on their heads to get to the other side!

Early explorers had no idea there was even more to marvel at. Something more valuable than gold lay right underneath their feet. Anyone could see the clean, clear water in the rivers and springs and streams. What they could not see were the Floridan and Biscayne Aquifers. This precious resource underground had been there for thousands of years. The aquifers spread from southern Alabama and Georgia all the way through to south Florida. Their depth varied from a few feet beneath the surface to 1,000 feet underground. Crystal-clear water was there, enough to supply the needs of animals and plants and humans for many years to come.

Natural Florida years ago was a breathtakingly beautiful place, but later generations had other ideas. They wanted farms and cities, not all that water on the ground. They wanted roads and highways and canals, not meandering streams.

The beauty was overlooked as men came to Florida to change it. Their thinking was "let's drain the swamp."

It is always dangerous to move quickly on a project without having all the facts. When Florida became a state and new settlers arrived by the hundreds, some of the rivers were cleared for steamboats. Homes were needed, so ancient forests were almost completely cleared. Businesses were encouraged, so land was cleared and drained for farms. Florida was growing, and fast. Better transportation was needed, so roads and canals would soon tear through the wild places.

It didn't take long to change the environment. Wild plants and animals were not considered. The destruction of habitat was not considered.

We, as Floridians, are very fortunate to have had three women—three Marjories—who showed us the damage that was being done. The three Marjories reminded us that the earth is fragile and that wild places need to be protected.

"In Wildness is the preservation of the world."
—Henry David Thoreau (1817–1862)[1]

Chapter 1

Before the Three Marjories

Florida stands out as unique among the other forty-nine states. A map shows clearly the shape of a long peninsula jutting more than 400 miles from temperate into tropical waters. The Atlantic Ocean is on its east side. The Gulf of Mexico is on the west side. Down south are the Straits of Florida and a chain of islands we call the Florida Keys. There are more than 1,300 miles of shoreline. No spot in the state is more than 60 miles from the ocean or the gulf.

Even the land in Florida is full of water. There are about 1,700 rivers and they are all sizes, all shapes. Many rivers in the northern part of the state are supplied by springs bubbling up from the ground. Those rivers naturally drained much of their water into other rivers flowing into the southern part of the state, now called the Everglades. When William Bartram saw the Suwannee River in Florida's early days, he called it "the cleanest and purest of any river" he had ever seen.[1]

Water, therefore, has always played a major role in Florida's history.

Changes started when Florida became the twenty-seventh state in the young United States on March 3, 1845. With new railroads and canals being built around the country, new Americans were on the move.

Many settlers went west, but some came south to Florida. They saw the beauty here, stayed, and told others about the wonders they had seen. Harriet Beecher Stowe came. She was the author of a book very popular at that time, *Uncle Tom's Cabin*. She and her husband built a house on the banks of the clean, clear St. Johns River. Steamboats took tourists right past her house in Mandarin. In 1873 she wrote a book, *Palmetto Leaves*, which told of the pleasant Florida climate, and she became one of the state's biggest boosters.

Ulysses S. Grant, after his two terms as president of the United States, took a steamboat ride on the Ocklawaha River. He was so impressed by the overhanging trees and the alligators sunning themselves on the banks

A day trip on a steamboat on the Ocklawaha River, 1900s. The river wasn't very wide! Courtesy of the State Library & Archives of Florida, Florida Memory.

that he remarked, "This is the greatest wonder I have ever seen."[2]

But the state was too wild for some. Many feared the Seminole and Miccosukee Indians. Although they had lived peaceably for years, the Indians were forced to move.

Many of the new settlers wanted to farm in the fertile soil, so plans to drain the water from the "worthless" swampland were considered. And some thought there was a need for better transportation across the state, so they started planning for a canal.

One group of Americans was left out of the decision-making, however. Men made the treaties and the boundaries for farms and the surveys for the drainage and canals. Men made the laws in Tallahassee, Florida's state capital.

Women in America were not allowed to vote, so they had no voice in politics. They were discouraged from getting a college education, unless they wanted to be a schoolteacher, nurse, or secretary. Women who completed high school were expected to marry, stay home, and raise their children. That was enough. Leave it to the men, thank you, to make the rules and get the work done.

What makes our three Marjories so fascinating is that they pushed the limits. All three graduated not only from high school, but from four-year colleges. Each earned honors in her academic studies. Two married, then divorced and lived on their own for years. The other married and became an equal partner to her husband; she was praised for her work, just as he was for his.

Each of our three Marjories came to Florida from different states, and they faced many hurdles. But their love for their adopted home was so strong that they stood up for their rights and the rights of generations to come. Two Marjories stood firm, with others, to protect the wild areas. The other wrote stories that would remind generations to come about Florida's wild backwoods and the fascinating people who had lived there. All three expressed their appreciation for the natural beauty of Florida in their own way.

They also saw dangers approaching. They were women, but they made sure their voices would be heard.

Chapter 2

Marjory Stoneman Douglas

Marjory Stoneman was born on April 7, 1890, in Minneapolis, Minnesota. At that time, there were only 42 states in the United States.

Marjory was the only child of Frank and Lillian Stoneman. Her parents opened her mind to beauty and learning while she was very young. Her mother played violin and guitar, so little Marjory learned to enjoy music. Her father always had books piled around the house, so his daughter soon was reading on her own. She loved stories and loved learning about her world.

Marjory was told about her relatives who had lived years before. Story after story was told to her with pride. One of her great-great grandfathers explored the oceans of the world. Her great-great uncle and aunt were Levi and Katie Coffin. They had risked their own lives to help enslaved people flee the South to seek freedom in the North. Levi and Katie were part of the Underground Railroad.

Her ancestors were brave people, and their stories taught little Marjory that each person, in his or her own way, can make a difference. If each person does something positive, then we'll create a better world for all. You just need to know that your goal is a good one, and then you can move ahead with enthusiasm!

Marjory loved to write, so she chose to be an English major at Wellesley College. However, when she took a geography class, she became absolutely fascinated with that subject also. She had so many questions. How were rivers formed? How deep were the oceans of the world? She had always loved the outdoors and the natural world, but suddenly she saw the whole earth with more insight and understanding. It gave her an even greater respect for the environment around her.

Marjory graduated from Wellesley with honors, but shortly after she arrived back home, her mother died of cancer. When a short marriage to Kenneth Douglas ended in divorce, she decided to make a new life for herself in south Florida. Her father, whom she hadn't seen in many years, was living in Miami. They were both anxious to see each other again.

She was twenty-five years of age. She bought herself a new dress for the journey and a one-way ticket south. Railroads were being built across America, so she rode to Jacksonville, Florida, and then took the new Florida East Coast Railway to Miami. Henry Flagler, a millionaire from New York, had completed his railroad track between Jacksonville and Miami just twenty years before.

She reached her station and couldn't believe her eyes. The sky was so blue and the clouds were so white and the sun was so bright! She later described her reaction with these words: "Above us was the enormous Florida sky. This was all a Florida that I'd no idea about. I was fascinated with the strange landscape that surrounded my new home."[1] Marjory Stoneman Douglas had found the place where she wanted to live.

There was a happy reunion between father and daughter at the station. Frank Stoneman had come south years before to start a newspaper in the growing city. His paper, small at first, would soon be named the *Miami Herald.*

It was at the *Herald* that Marjory would get more writing experience. She was asked to write the society column, which kept her very busy. She then went on to write "The Galley," for which she chose her own topics. Her father taught her well how to write for a newspaper: write what people want to know and also what they *need* to know.

Henry Flagler had completed railroad track from Jacksonville down the Atlantic coast all the way to Miami and beyond. He also built luxury hotels along the train route, from the Hotel Ponce de León in St. Augustine all the way down to the Hotel Royal Palm in Miami. As soon as winter winds started to blow in the north, rich visitors came south to enjoy the warm days, the warm water, and the elegant parties and balls held at these beautiful hotels.

Marjory wrote about the excitement happening in the bustling city, but she soon realized that there were also problems caused by so many people visiting or wanting to live in Miami. Land was cleared as quickly as possible to make room for more homes, more stores, and many more hotels. In 1920, Miami had only one skyscraper. Just five years later it had thirty under construction. The clear water of pristine Biscayne Bay was being polluted as construction went on close to the shoreline. The aquifer in that area was so stressed by so many people using water for drinking and bathing and watering lawns, that salt water soon crept in, making it unusable.

Marjory Stoneman Douglas on the steps of her home.
Courtesy of the State Library & Archives of Florida, Florida Memory.

Marjory remembered her relatives and how they had stood up for what they knew to be right. She was soon using "The Galley" to take a stand on a variety of issues.

In 1916, she was asked to travel with some other women to Tallahassee to talk with legislators about women having the right to vote. She described the trip in this way: "We could have been talking to a bunch of dead mackerel, for all the response we got."[2] Women continued to press for the vote, however, and by 1920, the Nineteenth Amendment was finally passed.

In 1923 Marjory left the very busy world of newspaper writing, wrote some stories, and decided to write a novel. But before she got too far, she was interrupted by an interesting request by the publisher of the Rivers of America Series. He asked her to write a book about a nearby river.

The book would include many facts and would involve a great deal of research. The fascinating geography class Marjory took in college came back to her mind. She agreed to write about the Everglades, just to the west of Miami.

She hadn't spent much time there yet, but the experiences she did have had been magical. She had gone with a friend to where workmen had been digging for the Tamiami Trail, and happened to witness the mating

Flock of white ibis, Dade County, Florida, 1981. Courtesy of the State Library & Archives of Florida, Florida Memory.

dance of the white ibis. The sight of so many of these beautiful white birds jumping up and down to attract a mate was something she would remember for the rest of her life. But what else was in that watery wilderness?

Chapter 3

The Everglades: River of Grass

Marjory Stoneman Douglas had been asked to write a book about a river. The Everglades sure didn't look like a river. Most of south Florida had water flowing over the land, but it had grass growing through it!

Early Spanish mapmakers labeled it "El Laguno de Espiritu Santo," or "Lagoon of the Holy Spirit." To them, it was a mysterious, sacred place.

The Indians living there called it "Pay-hay-okee." To them, it was "grassy water."

The author with a great interest in geography would find out the facts.

She went to people who had already been studying the subject for years. Garald Parker was a hydrologist at the US Geological Survey and was studying water and its flow. When Marjory asked questions, he tried to give clear, concise answers.

Can the Everglades be called a river?

Yes. It is water moving from one place to another.

But its flow is so slow. Grass can grow through it. May I then call it a river of grass?

Yes.

She had the title of her book!

Marjory asked many questions of many people. She read articles and books. She took many notes. She studied for five years to really understand her subject.

The Everglades. Photo by Steve Sammons.

She needed to put all the facts together so her readers would understand all the information she discovered in her research. Her writing would include scientific explanations of her subject, but she also wanted it to be easy for everyone to read.

Her opening sentence was: "There are no other Everglades in the world." And she ended that first paragraph by stating: "It is a river of grass." She knew her subject, and she understood the Everglades. She wrote clearly and carefully.

She told of how the natives living on the wet peninsula adapted to their natural surroundings. They built their homes up on stilts in watery areas. They hunted for food. They grew small gardens. They ate wild plants. Fires from lightning were a natural occurrence and helped clear out the small bushes and trees so that animals used for their food could be spotted more easily. Hurricanes and droughts were also natural occurrences. All living things at the time accepted what nature allowed.

Trees, too, had adapted to the watery land. Cypress trees, so plentiful around lakes, drop their seeds during the dry season because the small seeds cannot germinate in standing water. But when fully grown, cypress trees tolerate flooding better than any other tree in Florida. The river of grass was a thriving, living place!

Cypress trees. Photo by Steve Sammons.

In November of 1947, *The Everglades: River of Grass* was published. Marjory had succeeded in opening up many mysteries surrounding the glades. So many people were interested in learning about the area that all 7,500 copies of the first printing were sold out by Christmas. This was an important book!

Many people sent notes to Marjory to say how much they appreciated all her work in writing about the Everglades. One woman living in the central part of the state said the book would be excellent reading for "all readers concerned with . . . the great relations of man to nature."[1] That note was signed by Marjorie Kinnan

Rawlings, who was living in the backwoods of north central Florida and writing stories about the people who lived there.

The Everglades: River of Grass was important for people to read at that time. The Everglades was already being destroyed. The last chapter of Marjory's book is called "The Eleventh Hour." In it she states: "Perhaps even in this last hour, in a new relation of usefulness and beauty, the vast, magnificent, subtle and unique region of the Everglades may not be utterly lost."[2]

The Everglades: River of Grass became almost a bible for a new group of people: environmentalists. They understood that someone had to stand up and speak out about protecting our earth.

Her teachers at Wellesley College had taught Marjory Stoneman Douglas well. When she took on a serious project, she did her homework, she learned the facts, and although she may have stood only 5'2" tall, she spoke to everyone with authority.

Another important book she wrote was *Florida: The Long Frontier.* It told the whole history of the state she had come to love. The author again shared with her readers information they needed in order to understand their surroundings. As Floridians found when trying to tame the Everglades, mistakes can happen when moving ahead before gathering all the important information needed to make good choices.

Marjory became an expert on the Everglades and on Florida history. She lived to be 108 years old, and writing her book was just the beginning of her journey to save the Everglades from being "utterly lost."

Chapter 4

A History of the Everglades

When Florida was a new state, many people did not think of the Everglades as a river. They thought of it as a swamp, a wasteland, and good for nothing but draining. Pull a plug somewhere and drain the water so the land underneath could be used! One of Florida's first senators said he thought the entire region might drain so quickly that there might be a health hazard from all the dead fish that would be left on the dry land!

Native peoples had accepted the water along with the bounty it provided. Fresh fish, healthy animals, and plants had become a part of their diet and their way of living. New settlers had different ideas. They wanted farms, and those farms needed dry land. They wanted water—but only where they wanted it. The "excess" water had to go.

The best way to change something, however, is to understand it first.

There was a good reason why that water was there. The Everglades was part of a whole ecosystem that worked well when it worked naturally. Rivers as far north as Alabama, Georgia, and South Carolina flowed gently into rivers in the northern part of Florida. Some of this water kept flowing south into Lake Okeechobee. The name Okeechobee is a Miccosukee Indian word for "big water." When the big lake was full, it simply overflowed and the water continued on its way south, very slowly, out to sea.

Even an abundance of rain did not upset the system. Hurricanes or droughts were all tolerated as part of the natural workings of the area. It was when the natural system was tampered with that the problems began.

Not long after Florida became a state, millions of acres of watery land were sold to businessmen who promised to drain it. Big dredges were brought in. Channels were dug between one river and another.

Land to the south of Okeechobee was drained and used for large sugar and vegetable farms. But the farmers didn't want any more overflow from Okeechobee

Dredge "Culebra" for the Everglades drainage project, between 1915 and 1925. Courtesy of the State Library & Archives of Florida, Florida Memory.

during the rainy seasons. How would they hold back all that water? In the early 1920s, a dike, or levee, was built around the large lake. But when the natural flow was stopped, where was the overflow water to go? Channels were dug to take the excess to the east or the west, directly into the Atlantic Ocean or the Gulf of Mexico.

Nature fought back almost immediately. Two hurricanes came, in 1926 and in 1928, and took down the levee. The land and the farms were again flooded.

Florida author Zora Neale Hurston wrote a book called *Their Eyes Were Watching God*, in which she describes the devastation caused by hurricanes at that

Picking tomatoes on the Everglades, 1920s. Courtesy of the State Library & Archives of Florida, Florida Memory.

time. Thousands of laborers had been working on the farms and many lost their lives in the terrible floods.

The levee around Lake Okeechobee was not taken down. The US Army Corps of Engineers was called in to strengthen it. President Herbert Hoover, also known for the Hoover Dam in Nevada, had approved the project, so it was called the Herbert Hoover Dike. It was much stronger than before. The engineers thought that they finally had the water under control.

The water had certainly been stopped. Dikes and channels diverted much of the north-south natural flow of the water. The Tamiami Trail would change the flow of water farther south.

Henry Plant's railroad stopped in Tampa, on the west coast. Henry Flagler's railroad ran down the east coast to Miami, and then was extended all the way to Key West. Travel from Tampa to Miami would be very convenient— if a road were paved between the two growing cities. The Tamiami Trail (Tampa to Miami) was designed and built as a straight line across the Everglades. Again, it was built without regard for the flow of the Everglades or the wildlife living in the area. As digging proceeded to open the way for the highway, wildlife habitat was destroyed. After it was paved, animals trying to find safe habitat were killed by the thousands on the roadway. The animal population in that area decreased dramatically.

Again, Nature fought back. With the flow of water slowed or stopped, the hot Florida sun beat down upon the dried land. By 1936, the Everglades started to burn. The top layer of soil burned first, then down into the earth. Smoke billowed up from the land. It could be seen for miles. Animals were trapped. Even young Marjorie Harris could see smoke billowing into the air from the direction of the Everglades. She later recalled: "In the summers, the sky would glow with the Everglades burning."[1]

Aerial view of the Tamiami Trail cutting its way through the Everglades, 1960s. Courtesy of the State Library & Archives of Florida, Florida Memory.

The changes continued. More land was drained, even though a study done by the US Department of Agriculture showed that there were some wet areas that did not have the soil necessary for good farmland. The question then was: Why drain the whole thing? But more and more channels were built, with locks to control the flow of the water. The builders hoped that each "improvement" would finally tame the Everglades.

The story of the Everglades would not be complete without mentioning the jetport. In 1967 the airport in

Fire in the Everglades, 1927. Courtesy of the State Library & Archives of Florida, Florida Memory.

Miami was getting very busy. Many people were coming to south Florida, so a new airport—actually a jetport, for supersonic planes—was planned to be built in the Everglades! It would be in the middle of still-wild Big Cypress Swamp.

Supersonic jets would fly in and out, making loud booms that would frighten the wildlife living nearby. When finished, the jetport was expected to cover 39 square miles. Industrial buildings and a town would be built there; the increased traffic would require more roads and probably the widening of the Tamiami Trail between Tampa and Miami. It also would have cut off the flow of fresh water going to sections of Everglades National Park.

The builders worked quickly, building the first runway before anyone could oppose the idea. They didn't work fast enough. By 1969 the project was stopped.

In the 1960s and 1970s, the voices of environmentalists began to be heard. Some older groups, such as the League of Women Voters, the national and state Audubon Societies, and the Wilderness Society, had been speaking out for years for many causes. Other groups, like Marjory Stoneman Douglas's Friends of the Everglades, were formed to combat specific problems. Groups with a specific cause seemed to really make an impact.

Marjory Stoneman Douglas researched and wrote her book about the Everglades and warned her readers about the possible future for that grassy river. She thought the book might be enough, but when she saw the jetport being built, she was horrified.

She knew that some people were fighting against the building of the jetport, and she wished them well. When asked to speak to some politicians, she replied that she couldn't. She didn't think anyone wanted to listen to a seventy-nine-year-old lady! She said, "They won't listen to me. They'll only listen to groups." Her friend said, "Well, start a group!"

The Friends of the Everglades was formed. Marjory became its president—for almost twenty-one years. She once said, "I was hooked with the idea that would consume me the rest of my life."[2] Almost to her dying day she continued to try to convince anyone who would listen that the Everglades needed to be saved.

In 2000, the US Congress and the Florida legislature pledged $7.8 billion to fund a Comprehensive Everglades Restoration Plan. Our work goes on. . .

Environmentalists have said, "The Everglades is a test. If we pass, we may get to keep the planet."[3]

Chapter 5

Marjorie Kinnan Rawlings

When Marjorie Kinnan was born on August 8, 1896, in Washington, D.C., the United States was just over one hundred years old and was still growing. There were forty-five states in the Union. Western states were still being formed—Utah had become a state earlier that year.

The nation's capital was a busy place, but Marjorie's father owned a lovely, quiet farm in the nearby state of Maryland. Father and daughter spent many happy hours there. She learned to love the peace and beauty of natural places undisturbed by the hustle and bustle that was all around her.

She loved reading and writing, did well in school, and chose to go to college. She was accepted to the

Charles Rawlings and Marjorie Kinnan Rawlings. 1940s.
Courtesy of the State Library & Archives of Florida, Florida Memory.

University of Wisconsin at Madison, where she majored
in English. She did so well that she was selected as a
member of the local senior women's honor society on
campus. Working for the school literary magazine one
day, she met another writer, Charles Rawlings.

In 1919, they graduated, married, and started on their
paths to exciting writing careers. They moved from big
city to big city but didn't quite find what they wanted.
Charles's brothers were living in Florida, so they encouraged the young couple to move south.

Realizing they would have to support themselves until their writing would pay the bills, they bought an orange grove. Delicious Florida oranges could be sold at a good price in the northern states. Charles and Marjorie thought they could keep a farm going and sell citrus while they also worked at their writing.

The city folk bravely bought seventy-two acres in the backwoods of north-central Florida. It would be quite a challenge for them. Their old house had no indoor bathroom, just an outhouse a short distance from the house. They lived at Cross Creek, which got its name from its location between Orange Lake and Lochloosa Lake. They were four miles away from the small village of Island Grove. It was quite a difference from city life!

There were neighbors, not next door, but just close enough to hear if you shouted for help. And they would help when needed. They were families that had lived in the backwoods for generations, and had learned to rely on themselves and, occasionally, on each other.

They "made do." If they needed a new broom, they didn't go to a store. They cut a palmetto branch and trimmed the fronds to create a tool that would clean their homes nicely. Marjorie had never known people like this. She became fascinated by the way they lived.

Marjorie Kinnan Rawlings's home, Cross Creek, Florida, 1967.
Courtesy of the State Library & Archives of Florida, Florida Memory.

Charles and Marjorie cared for their farm animals and soon had fresh eggs each morning. They harvested from the old orange trees and planted new ones. Charles even built his wife a desk he made from the trunk of a palm tree so she could do her writing on the front porch.

While Marjorie was settling in to life in the backwoods, however, Charles had writing assignments that took him into the cities that were building up nearby. He soon chose to return to city life, so the couple separated and then divorced. Marjorie chose to stay alone at the farm.

Her neighbors living in those Florida backwoods were called "Crackers." The name may have come from their habit of cracking corn when they prepared their food. This was a whole new world for Marjorie. She soon realized that their way of life—and the backwoods—would not last much longer. Many people were coming to Florida, and towns and cities were being built, even in the deep woods.

Realizing that no one would know about these interesting people if their stories were not written down, Marjorie started listening closely. As her neighbors got to know her, they came to respect and trust her, so whenever they got together, they gladly shared stories about experiences they had through their years of living at Cross Creek.

Marjorie paid attention to every detail, even to their Cracker dialect, the distinctive words they used when they spoke to each other. In the chapter "My Friend Moe," in her book *Cross Creek*, Marjorie relates how Moe, one of her neighbors, explains their friendship: "Me and her is buddies, see? If her gate falls down, I go and fix it. If I git in a tight for money, she helps me if she's got it, and if she ain't got it, she gits it for me. We stick together. You got to stick to the bridge that carries you across."[1]

She listened closely to every word, and how it was said, and then went home to write the stories down in a notebook.

Marjorie was seldom alone. She had pets like Racket, the raccoon, who kept her company. There was never a dull moment when he was around. He could open the screen doors, even though she tried to keep him out. He entered the house whenever he wanted and ate anything in sight. He seemed to know when his favorite food was in the ice-box. As Marjorie explains it: "He could open all the ice-box doors. One day the colored iceman let out unholy shrieks. He had not noticed that the door of the ice compartment was ajar. He swung it open, and there sat Racket on top of a cake of ice, eating raw breakfast bacon."[2]

Marjorie kept very busy in spite of her little friends. Work on the farm still took much of her time, and she made time for her writing. She wrote some stories that were published in magazines, but she never had enough money to do more than pay the bills.

One day in 1933, Marjorie was tired of all the work and just had to get away for a while. She asked one of her neighbors, Dessie, to go with her on a boat trip up the St. Johns and the Ocklawaha Rivers.

Raccoon in the Florida Everglades, 1979. Courtesy of the State Library & Archives of Florida, Florida Memory.

Two women alone in a boat, with just a map and a compass, was a strange sight to the local people they passed. Today a boat trip on the St. Johns is easy, with many markers showing the way. But at that time, it was dangerous journey. Boats just followed the flow of the water, which opened into some large lakes—Lake Harney, Lake George, and Lake Monroe. Dessie and Marjorie weren't always sure which lake they were floating through! But it was just what Marjorie needed.

Seeing once again the beauty of the St. Johns and Ocklawaha Rivers reminded Marjorie of what she treasured about the wild backwoods. She loved this place. She would continue working at the farm. She would continue doing her writing. She had stories to tell.

One of her neighbors told her about a young deer his brother raised when they were young. It was a story of tenderness and yet a strength that comes as a young man matures. She started writing and worked very hard on getting the words exactly right. By the time she was finished, it was not a short story. It was a book. She called it *The Yearling.*

Chapter 6

The Yearling *and* Cross Creek

The Yearling was published in 1938, just a few years before America entered a dreaded second world war. Fear was in the air. But people reading *The Yearling* got a respite from their worries when they read about one year in the life of twelve-year-old Jody; his pet deer, Flag; and the Baxter family living in the untamed woods of Florida. There were dangers in the world and in the story, but there was also peace and hope within the pages of this special book.

"The Creek!" he shouted. "'He's tryin' to make the Creek!" Sound filled the swamp. Saplings crashed. The bear was a black hurricane, mowing down obstructions. The dogs barked and bayed. The roaring in Jody's ears was his heart pounding. A bamboo vine tripped him and he sprawled and was on his feet again. Penny's short legs churned in front of him like paddles. Slewfoot would make Juniper Creek before the dogs could halt him at bay.[1]

Life in the backwoods was a challenge. Just as we all have to face dangers in our lives, these families constantly had to deal with challenges. Old Slewfoot was a huge black bear that had been stealing pigs and whatever else he could get out of the farmyards in the area for years. All the neighbors had tried, but no one had yet been able to catch him. Penny Baxter and his son Jody went after this dangerous animal. They had to protect their food supply or they would have nothing to eat.

The woods held danger, but they were also places of wonder.

A spring as clear as well water bubbled up from nowhere in the sand. It was as though the banks cupped green leafy hands to hold it. There was a whirlpool where the water rose from the earth. Grains of sand boiled in it. Beyond the bank, the parent spring bubbled up at a higher level, cut itself a channel through white limestone and began to run rapidly down-hill to make a creek. The creek joined Lake George, Lake George was part of the St. Johns River, the great river flowed northward and into the sea. It excited Jody to watch the beginning of the ocean. There were other beginnings, true, but this one was his own. He liked to think that no one came here but himself and the wild animals and the thirsty birds.[2]

"Miz Rawlins," as her neighbors called her, had accepted both the danger and the beauty of the Florida backwoods.

It was Cal Long and his wife, Mary, who told Marjorie about Cal's brother and his pet deer. A boy having a deer for a pet would be unusual. Deer are wild animals, and a young one would take more food and care than the families in that area would have to spare. It was hard enough to find food for themselves sometimes. And there was not much time for pets. The garden and the barnyard animals needed to be tended, because they supplied food for the family. The hunting dogs needed special care so they could be ready to scare away bears or go out hunting for fresh meat. But to have a wild deer for a pet? That didn't happen often.

Marjorie realized this story was a special one. She spent many hours on her front porch with her typewriter, typing one page after another. If the words weren't right, she ripped out the sheet, threw it away, and tried again. She wanted to get every word right so that her readers would understand how important a pet deer was to this young boy in the woods.

She carefully described how his father, Penny Baxter, told Jody he could go back into the woods, to where the fawn's mother had just been killed, to try to find the baby deer. After much searching, Jody found the fawn in the midst of some thick palmettos.

> Movement directly in front of him startled him so that he tumbled backward. The fawn lifted its face to his. It turned its head with a wide, wondering motion and shook him through with the stare of its liquid eyes. It was quivering. It made no effort to rise or run. Jody could not trust himself to move.
>
> He whispered, "It's me."
>
> The fawn lifted its nose, scenting him. He reached out one hand and laid it on the soft neck. The touch made him delirious.[3]

Marjory Stoneman Douglas had to research the subject thoroughly for her nonfiction book on the Everglades. Marjorie Kinnan Rawlings had to do the same

Pair of fallow deer. Courtesy of the State Library & Archives of Florida, Florida Memory.

with her work of fiction. Ms. Douglas's book was true, full of facts, but Ms. Rawlings's book had to convey to her readers the feelings of her characters and to make almost real the place where her story happens. A good fiction writer can make you feel like you're there, watching the action going on.

Marjorie certainly knew the wildness of the place where Jody and the Baxters lived. Terrified of snakes before she moved to Cross Creek, she had actually come to enjoy seeing the king snake who had taken up residence by her front gate. He had his home there just as she had hers. They shared the property, and each respected the others' space. She could describe places and animals and people so well in her writing because she herself had seen them and respected them.

At one place in *The Yearling*, Marjorie even speaks of the unique crookedness of the Ocklawaha, the river she knew so well. Jody's father, Penny Baxter, is speaking with his neighbors, describing a hound dog that he wanted to trade with them. He told them outright that the dog was lazy and worthless, but the way he said it led them to think that the dog was an excellent hunting dog and that he was not telling the truth. Penny later admitted, with a smile, "My words was straight, but my intentions was crooked as the Ocklawaha River."[4]

All Marjorie's work was worth it. In 1939 she was awarded the Pulitzer Prize for fiction for *The Yearling*. In 1946, the story was made into a movie. The book and the movie brought her international fame. She finally had enough money to pay her bills, and she also received letters of congratulation from many readers, including one from Marjory Stoneman Douglas, living in Miami, Florida.

Marjorie Kinnan Rawlings wrote another very popular book. She called it *Cross Creek*. In it she introduces her readers to the people who actually lived there, using their real names and telling real stories about them. She described her own feelings about the place, calling it an "enchanted land." She had found something beautiful, something that had been there for years and years, although she had just discovered it. The people, the animals, the woods—all were so special. Her affection for Cross Creek came through in the words she carefully wrote.

Her readers would find it hard to ever just pass by a magnolia tree again after reading Marjorie's description of one at Cross Creek:

> The tree is beautiful the year round. It need not wait for a brief burst of blooming to justify itself, like the wild plum and the hawthorn. It is handsomer than most dressed only in its broad leaves, shining like dark polished jade. . . . The tree sheds some of its leaves just before it blooms, as though it shook off old garments to be cleansed and ready for the new. There is a dry pattering to earth of the hard leaves and for a brief time the tree is parched and

drawn, the rosy-lichened trunk gray and anxious. Then pale green spires cover the boughs, unfolding into freshly lacquered leaves, and at their tips the blooms appear. When, in late April or early May, the pale buds unfold into great white waxy blossoms, sometimes eight or ten inches across, and the perfume is a delirious thing on the spring air, I would not trade one tree for a conservatory filled with orchids.[5]

Philip S. May, Marjorie's friend and attorney, was so impressed with her stories that he wrote to her in 1947, saying: "Ponce de León discovered Florida in 1513, but he had found only the physical and material Florida. Then, more than 400 years later, you came to discover the heart and spirit of Florida and revealed them to the world in writings of rare beauty and sensitiveness."[6] His words state the truth about Marjorie Rawlings's writing.

Marjorie Kinnan Rawlings got married again, to Norton Baskin of St. Augustine. She then spent time with him there, but still returned when she could to her Cross Creek home. Unfortunately, Marjorie's life was short. She died at the age of fifty-seven, on December 14, 1953. She requested to be buried in a cemetery not far from her beloved Cross Creek.

But *The Yearling*, *Cross Creek*, and her other books and stories will live on. Young and old alike read and reread her work, and it takes them away from their busy lives to an earlier time in the beautiful Florida backwoods. She showed us "the heart and spirit of Florida" and untamed, wild Florida will live forever in the pages of her books.

Chapter 7

Saving the Wild Places

We are fortunate today that some of Florida's wild places have been saved in stories that will not be forgotten. We are also fortunate that special wilderness areas have been saved as parks. Many individuals and groups worked hard through the years to save at least some of wild Florida. Even before women had the right to vote and before the three Marjories started their work, groups such as the Florida Federation of Women's Clubs were working to save parts of Florida's environment.

In Florida's early days, when land was plentiful, many acres were given away. Some was given in exchange for promises that it would be drained. Some was given to encourage builders to create better transportation in the state. Railroad track was particularly needed.

When Henry Flagler built his railway all the way down the east coast of Florida, and then built large hotels along the way, he was not only helping meet the transportation needs but also building new businesses. He was given many acres of land, some of it around his railroad tracks, and some in the watery but precious Everglades.

Several people wearing strong boots actually ventured into the soggy Everglades, and they knew that some areas were too special to be drained or built on. In one particular spot, they found a very special habitat for many nesting birds and animals. There was high ground with palmettos, called hammock. It also had low, watery ground filled with gators in the grassy glades. They found a wide variety of native plants that were becoming endangered.

The Florida Federation of Women's Clubs was told about this area of great biological diversity and decided to work to help preserve it. FFWC members, and particularly their Preservation Committee chairperson, May Mann Jennings, the wife of one of Florida's governors, hoped to create Florida's first state park right there.

Since the land belonged to Henry Flagler, the FFWC asked Mary Flagler, Henry's widow, if she would consider donating some of the land for preservation. Mary, also an FFWC member, donated 960 acres. Realizing its value as special habitat, the state also donated 960 acres for a park, if the FFWC would maintain it.

That special place became Royal Palm State Park. It was dedicated in November of 1916, the same year that the US Congress authorized the National Park Service. In 1921, 2,080 more acres were added, creating a 4,000-acre state park.

Royal Palm would be Florida's only state park for about 20 years, and the only state park in the nation operated by the Federation of Women's Clubs. Royal Palm later became part of Everglades National Park.

Florida now has three national parks: Everglades National Park near Homestead; Biscayne National Park near Miami; and Dry Tortugas National Park near Key West. There are also more than 160 state parks and trails throughout the state.

Other protected areas are the national forests, such as the Ocala National Forest and Juniper Prairie Wilderness in central Florida, just to the east of the city of Ocala today.

Ocala National Forest was established in 1908. Some visitors come to see the hundreds of lakes and ponds. Some come hoping to see a black bear or panther or white-tailed deer on their walks through the woods. But many come to hike the Yearling Trail, which leads to where the movie version of *The Yearling* was filmed in 1946. The book is still being read and reread by young and old, and the Yearling Trail is heavily traveled by those who want to feel again the enchantment of those very special backwoods. Jody and his pet deer, Flag, will not be forgotten.

There are also preserves. Paynes Prairie Preserve State Park covers 21,000 acres in Micanopy, Florida, just south of the busy city of Gainesville. Marjorie Harris Carr, our third Marjorie, lived close to the preserve, and the Carr family helped to save the very special area.

The preserve includes the Paynes Prairie Basin, the main source of drainage for the Alachua Sink. During wet seasons, the basin can fill, like a bath tub, and suddenly the dry prairie is a lake. When it drains, it becomes meadow, or grassland, again.

This preserve contains diverse habitats for both wild and domestic animals. Bison had been seen by William Bartram many years before in this place, and they have been reintroduced here. There are horses and alligators. Nearly 300 species of birds have been spotted throughout the park. Paynes Prairie Preserve has been named a US National Natural Landmark.

There are also greenways. Marjorie Harris Carr was honored after her death when a greenway was named for her. She fought hard to save that land from destruction, so it was appropriate that she be so honored.

The Marjorie Harris Carr Cross Florida Greenway was created from land that was being used to build the Cross Florida Barge Canal. Marjorie and the Florida Defenders of the Environment saved the 110-mile corridor across central Florida from ruin. The canal would have cut Florida in two and destroyed the beauty of the still-wild parts of the Ocklawaha River.

The Greenway crosses central Florida from Yankeetown on the Gulf side to just south of Palatka, on the St. Johns River, on the Atlantic side of the state. Long (110 miles) and narrow (only 300 yards to a mile wide), the Greenway has trails through many habitats. Part of the Greenway is a National Recreation Trail, and therefore a part of America's national system of trails and greenways.

The Greenway has a wide variety of outdoor public recreation choices. Canoes and kayaks glide smoothly over the rivers and streams. Mountain bikers use the rough areas.

We need to preserve them all for future generations. Parks, preserves, greenways—all are critically important for the health of our children and grandchildren.

Kayaks on the water. Photo by Misty Sammons.

Marjorie Kinnan Rawlings wrote in her book *Cross Creek*:

We are bred of earth before we were born of our mothers. Once born, we can live without mother or father, or any other kin, or any friend, or any human love. We cannot live without the earth or apart from it, and something is shriveled in a man's heart when he turns away from it and concerns himself only with the affairs of men.[1]

Chapter 8

Marjorie Harris Carr

When Marjorie Harris was born on March 26, 1915, the United States of America was almost complete. There were forty-eight states in the Union, with Alaska and Hawaii still to join as the forty-ninth and fiftieth in 1959.

She was born in Boston, Massachusetts, but when Marjorie was three years old, the Harris family moved away from the cold northern winters. They bought an orange grove just south of Bonita Springs, on the banks of the Imperial River in sunny southwest Florida. Marjorie and her parents spent many happy hours exploring their wild 10-acre property and canoeing and fishing on the beautiful river.

Marjorie Harris at two years old, 1917. Photo by Mimi Carr.

Marjorie didn't always have to walk to do her exploring. She had her own little horse, a young mare named Chiquita. Chiquita was a Florida Cracker horse born on the Kissimmee Prairie. She had been caught and tamed there by cowboys!

To Marjorie, it seemed they had come to a wonderland. There were animals and plants that she had never seen before, and she was curious to learn all about them. The many books on her parents' shelves helped her understand the bugs and the critters around her. She found them all so fascinating that she wanted to learn more. Like the other two Marjories, she was absorbing a love and respect for her new home: natural, wild Florida.

Her parents assured her that many people loved natural things as she did, and told her about Ralph Waldo Emerson and Henry David Thoreau, two men who had written about the value of living with nature. Thoreau, however, also warned that men were endangering wild places. He inspired John Muir, who founded the Sierra Club in 1892. Muir then fought to save some of the western wilderness.

Marjorie soon found out for herself that some people did not have the same respect she had for living things. One day she realized there were fewer herons and egrets along the shore. She was told that men with rifles were shooting the beautiful birds so they could sell their feathers.

Called plume hunters, the men took the feathers to sell in large cities. It was the fashion of the day that women wore hats, and they would spend a lot of money for hats with delicate feathers decorating them. May Mann Jennings and others worked to educate women to stop buying that type of hat. A law was soon passed to make it illegal to have hats with plumes from these wild birds, but it was too late to save the many, many birds that had already been slaughtered.

In addition to the plume hunters, some men came to Florida with rifles to shoot the wildlife. They took steamboat rides on the beautiful rivers just to take aim at any anything that moved in the forests. Marjorie knew that some people living in the backwoods killed animals for their food, but "it was the stupidity of killing everything" that bothered her.[1] Again, it was women like Ms. Jennings and others who worked with the Florida Audubon Society to stop the slaughter of birds.

Marjorie attended the nearby elementary school, and the other students recognized that she was different. She definitely had a northern accent and she dressed for outdoor activities, usually wearing pants rather than dresses. She wore pants because she rode her horse, Chiquita, to school!

Small Florida towns in those days didn't always have a high school, so in 1928 the family moved from their farm to a larger town, Fort Myers. Four years later, Marjorie would have to move again, this time to attend college.

Women finally had the right to vote by that time, but after high school girls were expected to get married and have children. Few even thought of attending college.

Marjorie Harris had a thirst for learning more about the natural world around her. She had finished her basic schooling. Now she was determined to learn all she could about wildlife, even though there was no college nearby and no money for college tuition. Her father had died when she was 15, and her mother had to go back to work as a teacher. A teacher's salary would not pay Marjorie's college costs.

A small inheritance came just in time for her to register for the fall 1932 school year. Marjorie traveled north to Tallahassee, Florida's capital city. She registered at the Florida State College for Women (today's Florida State University) and declared her major as zoology, the study of animals.

She said very clearly, "My aim was to become a zoologist. I wanted to work with whole, live animals, preferably birds, in their natural surroundings."[2] She had a solid goal in mind and would work hard to reach that goal.

The inheritance money was soon gone, so Marjorie looked for work during the summer to pay her tuition for the next year. Fortunately, the National Youth Administration at that time would pay college tuition, and also room and board for the year, if students worked for them during the summer. The first year she worked in an office, which she did not enjoy, but the following years would be better.

She received permission to design a three-month summer field course that would teach preteens and teenagers about nature. The course plan was accepted, and she taught her program for her last two summers at college. Marjorie later said, "It was then that I became convinced that people will care for their environment if only they can learn a little bit about it."[3]

In four years, she proudly received her Bachelor of Science in Zoology. She had achieved such high grades that she was elected a Phi Beta Kappa scholar and invited into the science honor society, Sigma Xi. She was a woman and an honored scientist!

Again, she would push the limits of what women did in those days. She tried to find a graduate school, but even with her high grades and honors, she was denied admission.

When she was offered a job as federal wildlife technician at the Welaka Fish Hatchery, located near the St. Johns River, she broke tradition. She was the first woman in US history to be accepted for that position.

The work was interesting, and she eagerly learned about the native fish and the rivers nearby. She was particularly intrigued by one of the rivers, the Ocklawaha, which had many native fish in its waters and animals of many kinds made their homes near the banks of the meandering waterway. She fell in love with the beauty of the place, and that love would remain with her for the rest of her life.

She also found another love of her life when she traveled to the University of Florida to do some laboratory work. Since the university had only male students at that time, heads turned when a pretty young woman walked in the door. The word got around, but it was only when Archie Carr saw her that there was a mutual attraction.

Archie Fairly Carr Jr. was a graduate student at the university, and his major interest, too, was zoology. As they got to know each other, they realized they had a great deal in common. Their feelings for each other grew, and they both realized that they wanted to be together for the rest of their lives.

However, it was not a good time for marriage. Archie was working every minute of the day on his studies. Marjorie was dismissed from her job at the fish hatchery when she challenged a colleague who took credit for a discovery Marjorie had made. In an interview later, Marjorie mentioned that her supervisor was never comfortable working with a woman biologist. She took on a new job, but knew she would be dismissed again if her employers found out she was married. At that time, married women were expected to stay at home.

Nothing would hold back this couple. In 1937 they told Marjorie's mother that they were going to watch the moonrise over the Everglades, but they drove to another town where they asked a friend to marry them. When they arrived home, they told only a selected few about the marriage.

Archie went back to his studies. Marjorie worked at a marine station on Lemon Bay, near Englewood, Florida, several hours away from Archie. It was hard to be apart, but they dared not reveal that she was married. They needed the income from her work, and besides, she was an honors graduate of Florida State College for Women and wanted to continue working in science.

Six months later, Archie was awarded his doctorate from the University of Florida and Marjorie left her job. On June 11, 1937, Archie and Marjorie happily invited family and friends together to a ceremony that declared them husband and wife. Even though they had already been married for more than five months, the Christian ceremony that revealed the marriage was important to family. With Archie then a professor at the university, his wife was allowed to attend the (still all-male) graduate school at the University of Florida. Marjorie could

*Archie Carr and
Marjorie Harris
Carr, 1937.*
Photo by Mimi Carr.

finally again pursue her studies in zoology. She received her MS degree in 1942.

Marjorie and Archie both made wise choices in life partners as well as in their chosen fields of work. Because both of them had graduate degrees in zoology, they were soon accepted into the scientific community as a research couple.

Chapter 9

Archie Carr

Archibald Fairly Carr Jr. was born in the southern city of Mobile, Alabama, on June 16, 1909. That was just six years before Marjorie Harris was born in the northern city of Boston, Massachusetts. Archie and Marjorie became such partners in life that her story would not be complete without telling her husband's story.

Archie's childhood also prepared him for his life work of studying nature. He had many pets when he was young: lizards, turtles, snakes, frogs, and an armadillo were all part of his collection. He spent many hours just watching the way they ate and moved, and even how they reacted when he was around.

On a fishing trip in 1927, Archie became very ill with osteomyelitis in his right arm. Even after six operations, he was never again able to straighten that arm. But Archie would not let it hold him back from what he wanted to accomplish.

He was a very good student throughout school, finishing his formal education at the University of Florida. He was awarded his BA in English in 1932, his MS in zoology in 1934, and then his PhD in biology in 1937.

Archie had excellent teachers. His professors did not teach only from books. Since they were studying animal life, they stressed the importance of learning the animal's place in the natural world and how it lived in its own home environment. The students took many field trips around the state, so they could actually see the animals living naturally.

Archie Carr, like his wife Marjorie, knew what he wanted to accomplish in life. He wanted to study turtles. When he was asked, toward the end of his life, why he chose that particular subject, he said, "I just liked the look on their faces. There is an old, wise . . . look about turtles that fascinates people."[1]

This fascination with his subject led Archie to become an expert in sea turtles. There are seven species of sea turtles. Not much research had been done before about their nesting habits, so Archie started tagging some turtles and amazed many other scientists by determining how far the turtles would travel to nest and lay their eggs. Once he found that the turtles went as far as the shores of Africa, Costa Rica, Honduras, and other places in the world, he traveled to those countries and worked with scientists there in order to help protect the turtles at their nesting times.

He had plenty of help with his work. His brother Tom, a physicist at the University of Florida, was a great help in tagging turtles so they could be tracked on their journeys. Environmentalists in many other countries were eager to work with Archie. His college students caught their professor's passion for his subjects, and many worked with him, wherever he went. After their college studies, many of his students also went on to do their own research to preserve sea turtle habitats.

Archie became an expert on turtles, so he was asked to write a book on the subject. His *Handbook of Turtles: The Turtles of the United States, Canada, and Baja California* was published in 1952. The book added so much new information about the subject that he was awarded the very prestigious Daniel Giraud Elliot Medal by the National Academy of Sciences.

Archie wrote 11 books and more than 120 scientific articles in his very busy lifetime. He has been called the "world's greatest authority on turtles and a pioneering conservationist."[2] He wrote not only for other scientists, but also for general readers, who caught his fascination with these ancient-looking creatures.

Over the years he wrote about many subjects in nature. Marjory Stoneman Douglas had written her book on the Everglades years before, but Archie was asked to write another, more than 25 years later. There was definitely interest in that subject. People were still curious about that grassy river!

One of Carr's 11 books was *The Windward Road: Adventures of a Naturalist on Remote Caribbean Shores*. It was published in 1956 and won two major writing awards. *Mademoiselle* magazine took a chapter of that book, called "The Black Beach," and published it as a short story. It won the O. Henry Prize for short-story writing. Since he could write not only for scientists, but also for any interested readers, he was awarded the John Burroughs Medal from the American Museum of Natural History for his nature writing.

Archie Carr was an expert on sea turtles and how they lived, but he also helped save their habitat. He was one of the first to speak out on the imminent danger to their survival. Ecology—a new concept—was becoming popular. People were finally realizing that the whole earth is just one entity. Everything on earth depends on everything else. People were realizing that when a species becomes endangered, it is a warning to all of us.

Sea turtles go back to their same nesting sites year after year. Knowing that, people would steal the freshly laid eggs or the turtles themselves. Both fetched a good price at markets around the world. If too many were taken, however, the sea turtle population would become endangered.

The Caribbean Conservation Corporation (recently renamed the Sea Turtle Conservancy) was created to help save habitats for nesting sea turtles. Archie served as its technical director, even addressing simple fixes such as keeping shorelines dark at nesting season. If there are lights on the beach, the little sea turtle hatchlings coming out of their shells might move toward the light instead of the surf.

In Costa Rica, Archie established and directed the Green Turtle Research Station at Tortuguero on the Caribbean coast. It is now called the John H. Phipps Biological Field Station. The word *tortuguero* is Spanish for "region of turtles." In 1975, the Costa Rican government established Tortuguero National Park, a twenty-mile stretch of beach where turtles were safe to make their nests. Archie also developed a school of biology at the

University of Costa Rica, and it became one of the best of its kind in Central America.

Archie's trips in Florida or to Honduras or Costa Rica often included Marjorie and even their children. Archie and Marjorie Carr had much more than a marriage. Theirs was a true partnership. She worked with him on turtle research and he supported her work in the campaign to save the Ocklawaha River and Paynes Prairie. A friend once said, "Of his many collaborations, one of Archie's most satisfying must have been with his wife of more than thirty years."[3] It was 30 years when he wrote that, but Archie and Marjorie spent 50 years together as husband and wife before Archie died. It had been a good partnership indeed!

Honors came from many places. The University of Florida honored him when the Archie Carr Center for Sea Turtle Research was established there in 1986. Their esteemed professor, a member of their university staff, had gained an international reputation in the field of sea turtle research not just for himself, but also for his university.

About two weeks before Archie died, however, he received one of his greatest honors. He received the Eminent Ecologist Award from the Ecological Society of America in 1987. It was a prestigious award, indicating to the world the high regard his colleagues had for Carr's work. Since he was too ill to attend a ceremony, they brought the award to him at his bedside.

After a long, busy life, Archie died peacefully at home in Micanopy on May 21, 1987.

Marjorie didn't stop working. She put together one last book about Archie's work in Florida and his love of the state. She called it *A Naturalist in Florida: A Celebration of Eden.* It's a fascinating tribute to her husband's life.

The awards didn't stop with Archie's passing. The University of Florida's Presidential Medal, its highest honor, was awarded to Archie Carr. The Archie Carr National Wildlife Refuge in Florida and the Dr. Archie Carr Wildlife Refuge in Costa Rica were named for him. An Archie F. Carr Medal at the University of Florida was created to honor other biologists and their work.

Sea turtles today survive in large part because of Archie Carr. Threats to turtles have grown, but there are now many scientists and organizations working for their long-term survival.

The pioneering ecologist Rachel Carson wrote, "Those who dwell, as scientists or laymen, among the beauties and mysteries of nature, are never alone or weary of life."[4]

Chapter 10

Two Working Together

Marjorie and Archie Carr both loved Florida and its natural environment. The home they chose in 1949 was witness to their love of wilderness. Although they traveled a lot, home was just south of Gainesville, near the small but historic town of Micanopy. Twenty-five acres were farmland and the rest of their 200 acres remained wild. The woods contained lakes and swamps, and the Carrs loved walking around their property. They saw something new almost every day.

On exploring the property, they found a sinkhole that made a small pond, and on its shore, they built their house. They named the pond Wewa, the Seminole Indian word for water. From their living room window, they had a great view of all the animals and birds that visited their little pond. Herons and egrets, frogs and turtles, ducks and gallinules, alligators and even a bobcat either settled there or took a sip of the water before traveling on.

Some became family friends. Jasper, the alligator snapping turtle, took up residence there. Archie just needed to dangle a piece of meat over the water and Jasper would come up out of the water to be fed. A female alligator that lived in the pond for forty years had to find her own dinner!

Some wild things even came into the house. An otter they named Jim thought he was part of the family. He lived in the house and learned to swim in the toilet bowl. He had his own pool outside but loved to play in the toilet. Once Archie found him there, head down, playing in the water. He gently closed the lid on him and went into the living room to read. A few minutes later, Jim rushed in, soaking wet, and bit him! All was soon forgiven, because he continued to accompany the family on walks and jump into a stream to swim until they were all ready to return home.

Archie and Marjorie enjoyed all this with their children. They had one girl and four boys who learned to love nature as their parents did. They had creatures surrounding them and lots of books to learn from.

Their home was a peaceful place, but always busy. Marjorie and Archie would work at home on writing or other projects, so they purposely built a long driveway approaching the house. If Archie was in the middle of his writing and didn't want to be disturbed, he had time to escape out a side door and continue working. Marjorie and the children would entertain the guests!

The five children learned so much by living by Wewa Pond. They helped out with farm chores, taking care of

Marjorie Carr at the shore with her children, 1953. Photo by Mimi Carr.

the donkey, two milk cows, a small herd of Hereford beef cattle, one pig, and a small flock of Rhode Island Red hens. The children were sometimes driven to school in a truck with cattle in the back! As often as she could, Marjorie also took the children on trips to see other wild places in Florida.

With their love of wilderness, Archie and Marjorie noticed that there were jobs to be done.

Marjorie took her children to nearby Paynes Prairie, which was one of the places that she and her husband would help to preserve. Her children loved running over the wide expanse of land when they were young, but when a road cut through it, and through the Carr's property, Marjorie took action.

The prairie's rich history went back to the 1700s when William Bartram saw the wild beauty of the place. The Seminole Indians had lived there in peace for years. It was such an interesting place. It was normally a wide prairie, what William Bartram called the Alachua Savanna, but when heavy rains caused the area to flood in 1871, it looked like a lake for about twenty years.

The lake was drained in the early 1900s and the dried land was rented out to cattlemen. With cattle on the land, fences went up, and the animal and plant life that had lived there for years could no longer survive. That hurt the environment, but in 1964 an interstate highway, I-75, cut through part of the prairie—and also took part of the Carrs' property.

Marjorie and the Gainesville Garden Club got to work, and the prairie that was left was saved. By 1970 the Florida Department of the Environment called it Paynes Prairie Preserve, the first of many wild areas they would later save.

With her children in school, Marjorie had time to take on other challenges to her local area. For years the main street of Micanopy was lined with very old live oak trees, with graceful Spanish moss hanging from their branches. Some people suggested getting rid of the "messy" trees, but thanks to Marjorie and others, the live oaks and the old historic buildings in what is now the Micanopy Historic District, were saved.

Marjorie and Archie both had their eyes wide open to the threats around them. When some people did not value the history and the environment in the area, Marjorie and Archie together spoke up to remind them of its importance.

They learned that a road was to be built right through the middle of the University of Florida campus. Roads were important then because the university was growing fast. But this road would take away a part of Lake Alice,

Governor Claude Kirk presenting award to Marjorie Carr while her husband, Archie Carr, looks on, 1970. Courtesy of the State Library & Archives of Florida, Florida Memory.

a lake that had been there for years. Lake Alice (formerly known as Jonah's Pond) was still a place where native birds and alligators made their homes. It was a place of respite from the busyness of campus life.

Plans for the road were already underway when the professors realized it would change the precious lake. Archie, Marjorie, and many others worked to convince the state of Florida and the university that Lake Alice was needed where it was, as it was. The building of the highway was canceled.

Whether in Florida or out of the country, Marjorie and Archie worked together. She helped him with his turtle research while in the Central American country of Honduras. Being very interested in birds, Marjorie also went off into the rain forest to do her own research on the magnificent birds of that country. After their separate adventures, they would come together again, share what they had learned, and write down their findings. Marjorie became such an expert on the birds of Honduras that she

Marjorie and Archie in a dugout canoe called a cayuca with Archie's biologist friend, Larry Ogren. Rio Tortuguero, Costa Rica, 1970. Photo by Mimi Carr.

eventually prepared a catalog with information about each bird she had seen.

Marjorie and Archie lived at a time when information about our natural environment was needed in our world. They did pioneering research on several subjects, helping conservationists around the world to understand the dire need for active participation in just causes.

The study of ecology was a new science, and the public was just becoming aware that parts of their environment were being destroyed. As more people understood the dangers around them, they followed in the footsteps of the three Marjories and Archie Carr. People realized they, too, needed to take responsibility for the preservation of their own natural environment.

It was passion for the subject that was important. Marjorie Carr once said, "The first time I went up the Ocklawaha, I thought it was dreamlike. It was a canopy river. It was spring-fed and swift."[1] Passion for the natural beauty around them and the struggle to keep our earth healthy is necessary for environmentalists even today. They know they have an obligation to save our planet for future generations.

"Once wilderness is gone, it is gone forever."
—*Marjorie Harris Carr*[2]

Chapter 11

A Canal across Florida

Living things on earth are dependent on each other, but before the study of ecology, not much thought was given to that concept. In 1962 Marjorie Harris Carr was stunned by the news that a Cross Florida Barge Canal was being built across Florida and it was planned to cut through a section of the Ocklawaha River.

The enchantingly beautiful and wild Ocklawaha River that she had seen years earlier would be severely affected. The canal planners were not considering the beauty of the Ocklawaha or the canal's impact on the habitat surrounding the river. Marjorie and others were amazed—and horrified.

The idea of a canal certainly was not new. It went back to the days of Pedro Menéndez de Avilés, who founded the colony at St. Augustine in 1565. Menéndez sailed up and down 400 miles of Atlantic coastline hoping to find a water route through the long peninsula. He wanted to reach the Gulf of Mexico without sailing around the treacherous Straits of Florida at the southern tip.

By the 1820s some surveys for a canal had already been completed. Canals were being built in other states. The Erie Canal was built in 1825 and was very successful, making travel much easier for new settlers to travel west.

The idea of a ship or barge canal was still simmering when Florida became a state in 1845. Some clearing had been done on Florida's rivers to allow steamboats to barely clear the river banks, but that clearing had not destroyed the surrounding environment. By 1852 that would change. More surveys were done for a cross-Florida canal, all of which would change the landscape of central Florida.

The American Civil War (1861–1865) put a stop to any building, but after the war, there again was money to spend. Many people had heard about the beauty, the sunshine, and the cheap land, and they came to Florida in droves. Railroads that were spreading out all over

America had also come to Florida. Henry Plant built a railroad line to Tampa. Henry Flagler built his railroad line down the Atlantic coast. It was easier to reach most places in Florida, but businessmen wanted a canal across the state.

By 1930, twenty routes were under consideration, and finally a decision was made. They chose "Route 13-B" which went from Yankeetown on the Gulf through several rivers, including the Ocklawaha River Valley, through to the St. Johns and the growing city of Jacksonville.

The proposed canal through central Florida would accommodate ships, not just barges. Ships needed a depth of 35 feet, whereas barges would only have needed a depth of 12 feet. No thought was given to the rivers that would be totally scarred and to the possible danger to the aquifer under the ground. There were not enough jobs at the time for those who needed them, so in September of 1935 President Franklin Delano Roosevelt allowed this project to begin.

Marjory Stoneman Douglas had made it quite clear. There was a very good, very solid reason for the Everglades to be a "river of grass." That river worked very well when left alone. The Ocklawaha and other rivers in north central Florida also were not only breathtakingly beautiful, but they were clean and smooth running, when they were not changed by men.

But men were determined to change the natural flow of Florida's rivers for their own purposes. There would be a ship canal.

Work was stopped several times because of lack of funds and some opposition was heard. The people speaking against the route of the canal were those who had learned more about the uniqueness of Florida's animals, forests, and people.

Some had read Marjorie Kinnan Rawlings's book *The Yearling*. It was popular and widely read, especially after she was awarded a Pulitzer Prize for her story. A movie was then made from the book, and many people actually saw the place where Jody might have lived. It was filmed in the Big Scrub, the backwoods of Ocala National Forest, and showed clearly the beauty, and the terror, of Florida's untamed backwoods.

Zora Neale Hurston, another Florida author, was known for her stories about another part of central Florida. She was African American, and she had been born and brought up in Eatonville, near Orlando. What made Eatonville different and special was that it was governed by African American men, highly unusual at the time. Zora, in her own writing style (she also wrote in dialect when her characters spoke), tells of the wonders of growing up in such a loving, peaceful town.

And in 1947, Marjory Stoneman Douglas's book *The Everglades: River of Grass* was published. She opened up the mysterious Everglades for her readers and they came to understand that the large wet area in south Florida was not just swamp. It was natural habitat for people, animals, and birds, and a necessary part of the flow of water through the state. When Everglades National Park was opened, people went to see for themselves the beauty of that environment.

Unfortunately, the canal excavation through central Florida did not stop. It continued, on and off, until the 1960s and 1970s, when the problems the engineers were facing became even more apparent. The drainage of the Everglades in south Florida also continued. Yes, there was an Everglades National Park, which saved a portion of the watery wilderness, but it was endangered. Not enough fresh water was allowed into the park because the engineers had stopped the natural flow. A drought in the early 1960s caught the men in charge of water management off guard.

Even this saved portion of the Everglades might have dried up and burned, but the engineers in charge immediately opened some channels. With the natural flow gone, they had to be vigilant so that water got to where it was needed, but only when it was needed. It was a constant threat to the life of the park.

Man's control of the environment was changing much of America. Bison in the Midwest of our country had roamed freely for years. Fences cut them off from their ranges, and many were killed. Native Americans who tried to protect land they had used for generations were expected to live on reservations. Large dams were built in many states to stop the flow of rivers, creating reservoirs of water for new cities being built.

Slowly but surely, however, new voices were heard. Questions were asked about the canal and the drainage in the Everglades. Funding was finally stopped for a ship canal, and when work started again, the project became a barge canal. Even so, the rivers and the aquifer would still be affected.

The questions kept coming. Railroads and roadways had already been built. Why was there a need for a barge canal? And wasn't the preservation of the rivers and aquifer just as important as a water route across Florida? And as for the drainage in the Everglades—how much drainage was enough?

Environmentalists spoke out. Unfortunately, part of the Ocklawaha River was on the planned route of the

Construction work on the Cross Florida Barge Canal. 1950s.
Courtesy of the State Library & Archives of Florida, Florida Memory.

barge canal. It seemed there was no way to change that. There was no group in central Florida strong enough to pressure the businesses and politicians to change that decision. Part of the Ocklawaha River would no longer run free.

> *"The salvation of the Florida scene will come about only if the public savors its beauty, understands its limitations, and speaks up for its preservation."*
> —*Marjorie Harris Carr*[1]

Chapter 12

Florida Defenders of the Environment

All rivers are special in their own way, but so many people recognized the value of the Ocklawaha that it was designated as one of 63 outstanding rivers in America. Its name comes from a Creek Indian word meaning "muddy water." The water itself is crystal clear, but it gets its light brown color from the many trees at its edge. It is part of a floodplain forest, and one of the last homes of the black bear and the panther in the state. The river is narrow, it's shallow, and it winds back and forth. It is also one of the few rivers in North America that flows north, like the St. Johns.

And now its flow was to be changed forever by a barge canal.

Marjorie Carr was a very busy wife and mother, and she was speaking out about other challenges near their home. But she could not allow this to happen to her beloved Ocklawaha. She became determined to take on this cause as well. Someone had to speak out against those who would ruin such a treasure.

She was a trained, seasoned scientist. She put her emotions aside and studied every aspect of her subject. She already knew a lot about the fish in that river, since she had worked in a fish hatchery near there years before. She especially knew the largemouth black bass, since she had done much research on the black bass for her postgraduate degree at the University of Florida. Birds, turtles, and snakes lived on the river's shores. Alligators sunned themselves peacefully on fallen tree trunks. Many people loved this river, so she knew she would have help.

She worked with the Alachua Audubon Society, which she cofounded in 1960. Thinking that the barge canal would definitely be built across Florida, she and her fellow activists simply wanted to change the route of the canal. She didn't want it to ruin the Ocklawaha.

They decided to alert the public to what was happening. The Audubon Society planned a program to be held on November 8, 1962, to which the public was invited. The program presented was called "The Effects of the Cross Florida Barge Canal on Wildlife and Wilderness." Some in the audience were convinced that the problem was serious, but more voices were needed.

Groups in nearby towns were also concerned, and by 1964, their voices got louder and stronger. They had no formal office. When they met at Marjorie's home, her kitchen table was covered with papers. There was serious talk about plans for saving the Ocklawaha, but all of the members also helped to fold letters and put stamps on envelopes. Even her children helped out when they could.

Marjorie wrote a letter to the president of the United States, and to his wife, Lady Bird Johnson, hoping they would listen. She talked with politicians and businessmen. She cornered anyone who would listen. A woman talking to male politicians was still hard to do, so Marjorie sometimes called herself a "housewife from Micanopy" to get their ears, and then proceeded to surprise them with her knowledge of the subject.[1]

Construction of the canal had been stopped for two decades, but in 1964, President Lyndon Baines Johnson allowed the Army Corps of Engineers to start construction again. By 1966, while Marjorie's group was still hard at work, the engineers brought in huge machines like the "crusher-crawler" to start work on the Ocklawaha. Part of the gently flowing river was changed into a reservoir called the Rodman Dam. The dam was to help control the water going through the barge canal. By 1968, 5,000 acres of beautiful forest had been destroyed. It was done without any consideration for the environment, its beauty, and its wildlife.

It was no longer possible to save the free-flowing Ocklawaha. Construction had gone too far. The goal now was even larger and harder to achieve. They needed to stop the building of the canal totally, before it ruined ecosystems all across the state. Was it possible? It would be hard to defeat a project proposed by the US Army Corps of Engineers, and this one was already underway.

The active and determined group needed a name that would be remembered, and it needed an office. In July of 1969, the Florida Defenders of the Environment (FDE) was born, and the members leaped into action. Their task was to work as quickly as possible, but very scientifically and thoroughly, before any further damage could be done to other lands and rivers in the way of the canal.

The evidence for their cause needed to be very clear and very scientifically based. True, the whole Ocklawaha River Valley was an ancient treasure known for its beauty and its bounty. But it was also one of only 68 wild rivers left in the whole nation. It was another treasure that was soon to be lost!

Also lost would be the biological diversity of the woods and streams in and around the river. For decades, professors from the University of Florida had taken their graduate students to the Ocklawaha. These field trips taught students how plants and animals lived in their natural habitat. It was getting harder and harder to find undisturbed places like this. The Ocklawaha River regional ecosystem was rare and needed to be protected.

The group published their findings in a very important 115-page pamphlet called *The Environmental Impact of the Cross Florida Barge Canal with Special Emphasis on the Ocklawaha Regional Ecosystem*. They had to convince people that rivers flowing naturally are necessary to the health of the ecosystems where they live.

The authors of the impact statement were noted scientists and laypeople, including Archie Carr. The writing was so clear and easy to understand that the statement was understood by laypeople and scientists alike. It was one of the first of its kind and became a model for many others also fighting for environmental causes in the future. The fight to save the Ocklawaha was no longer a regional or even a state fight. The FDE was making it a national fight. The FDE asked for help from the US government.

With their scientific proof in writing, the next step was a big one: a lawsuit. On September 16, 1969, the Environmental Defense Fund filed a legal suit against the builders of the canal, the Army Corps of Engineers, in the US District Court in Washington, D.C., on behalf of the Florida Defenders of the Environment. They insisted that construction be totally stopped until the builders could prove they were not destroying the environment. They also stated very clearly that citizens have rights to the environment in which they live. These rights cannot be violated by the government or by private businesses. This was a revolutionary idea at the time.

They gave clear, scientifically based predictions as to what would happen to the whole area if the barge canal across the state were completed. Plants, animals, and humans would all be affected negatively by the changes to the ecosystems along the route. The aquifer could very well be harmed, since construction could cause fractures in the limestone under the surface. Pollutants could leak into the precious aquifer. And an interstate highway system and railroads already crossed Florida. How much need was there now for a barge canal?

The Army Corps of Engineers was seldom questioned about changes it was making all over America, but this time it needed to come up with answers. Finally, it had to admit that it had not done any studies on the environmental hazards to land and wildlife along the path of the canal. Before this time, it had simply decided on a path and started building.

The Florida Defenders of the Environment had science and strong facts on their side. And they made their point. The canal building would stop.

In his State of the Union address in 1971, President Richard M. Nixon called upon Americans to "make our peace with nature."[2] He halted construction of the canal "to prevent potentially serious environmental damage."[3]

Environmentalists were no longer afraid to speak up. The very first Earth Day was celebrated on April 22, 1970. Twenty million people participated in the event by planting trees or just celebrating the wonders of our planet.

Marjorie and the Florida Defenders of the Environment watched closely the other news around Florida. The jetport proposed for the Everglades, which was started so quickly in 1967, was defeated by 1970. When citizens spoke loudly and had facts to back up their voices, legislation was finally passed to help protect the environment in many states.

In 1969 the National Environmental Policy Act was passed, requiring an environmental impact statement, like the one the FDE had written, before any federal monies could be used on building projects. This was a major step toward protecting the health of the earth.

The Florida Defenders of the Environment had their victory. Work on the barge canal had been stopped after only a third of the project was complete. The land set aside for the canal would be set aside for recreational use and would be called the Cross Florida Greenbelt State Recreation and Conservation Area. Marjorie Carr was on its advisory board.

Marjory Stoneman Douglas, still speaking out to save the Everglades in south Florida, was well aware of the fight to save the Ocklawaha in north central Florida. She sent a message to Marjorie Harris Carr, saying, "I know you will not rest easy until the final word is said . . . but surely all the preliminaries for success are at hand."[4]

But there was still more to be done. The work on the canal had been stopped, but there was nothing officially signed by either the state or federal governments. Legally, the project could have been revived. It was not until the presidency of George H. W. Bush, who was interested in environmental causes, that a bill was finally signed into law on November 28, 1990. There would be no cross-Florida canal. The Florida government also made the decision final on January 22, 1991.

This was a huge relief for Marjorie and the FDE. Marjorie Carr said at the time, "I think elected officials listen to the public, if the public speaks loudly. . . . And the rascals will get turned out if they are perceived as neglecting the environment."[5]

But again, there was one more very important step to take. The Rodman Dam still blocked the flow of the Ocklawaha River. The Ocklawaha needed to run free again so that the manatees, the bass, and other fish and animals would again have clear passage on their migratory routes. For the rest of her life, Marjorie Carr and the FDE worked to get the dam taken down.

Marjorie and the FDE met with state legislators in December of 1976 and after much talk there was some hope that the dam would be removed. There was even a suggestion that the Ocklawaha be designated a "wild and scenic river." President Jimmy Carter in 1977 recommended tearing down the dam and restoring its natural flow. It did not happen.

In 1998, despite all the efforts made to restore the river, the Rodman Dam was still there. Another dam, the Eureka, had been built but had never been finished, so that was not as big a problem as the Rodman. The Rodman, also called the Rodman Reservoir, had become a very popular fishing spot, and businesses near the dam did not want to give it up. The only change they would make is changing the name to the George Kirkpatrick Dam to honor one who fought hardest to save it.

The fight had continued for over 40 years. Even at 82 years of age and terminally ill, Marjorie Harris Carr still spoke out for her beloved Ocklawaha River. She also helped many others with their own environmental concerns. She hoped to see other rivers freed. The Apalachicola, Suwannee, Wekiva, and St. Johns all needed help. She even had hope that the Everglades would be restored some day.

Although very sick, Marjorie made her bedroom into an office, with a filing cabinet and telephone right by her bed. But the Rodman Dam would not be taken down in her lifetime.

Marjorie Harris Carr died on October 10, 1997, in Gainesville, Florida. She had lived in her beloved Florida for almost 80 years. She had worked hard to preserve parts of it for almost half her life. People praised her work with the Florida Defenders of the Environment. She was called "Our Lady of the Rivers" and "one of the true pioneers of the movement to preserve what is best about Florida."[6]

Almost 300 people attended her funeral service. The sadness was broken with smiles when the hearse drove off to the cemetery. On the back of the black hearse was a bright green and white bumper sticker that said, "Free the Ocklawaha River."[7]

Less than one year later, in May of 1998, the Florida legislature passed a law naming the Cross Florida Greenway after Marjorie Harris Carr.

"The key to success in any conservation effort is to get the facts—and then act. Get all the possible information pertaining to all the different aspects of the problem, making sure to differentiate between facts and someone's opinion or interpretation of those facts."—Marjorie Harris Carr[8]

Chapter 13

Accomplishments of the Three Marjories

Marjory Stoneman Douglas has been called "the Grand-mother of the Everglades." She put on what she called her "fighting hat" and spoke out, loud and clear, against the destruction of the wet, fascinating south Florida landscape. When she wrote her book *The Everglades: River of Grass*, she thought she had done enough to make people aware of the dangers to that environment. Little did she know at the time that she would spend the rest of her 108 years on earth fighting to save that river.

Marjory Stoneman Douglas also wrote books for young readers. In those stories she also was teaching her

Marjory Stoneman Douglas, 19??. Courtesy of the State Library & Archives of Florida, Florida Memory.

younger audience about the history of Florida, the state she had come to know so well.

Two of her books, *Freedom River* and *Alligator Crossing*, are about young boys and the challenges they face while growing up in early Florida. Marjory was so skilled at writing that once a young reader started one of her stories, they would want to keep on reading.

His fearful glance was caught up high by moving white birds' wings. The emptiness was real. But as if he could not believe it, his heart within his bony chest shook him with its pounding. He tried to stand up and look behind him, half cringing. . . . His head rose. He breathed deeper. His wide lips widened into a grin. He was alone.[1]

Marjory Stoneman Douglas had the courage of her ancestors. She spoke up for what she believed in. She made a difference through her work with the Friends of the Everglades. She taught young people about the history of her fascinating state. The Friends of the Everglades is still active today, and her books for adults and young readers can still be found in most public libraries.

Marjorie Kinnan Rawlings, unlike the other two Marjories, was not an environmentalist. She wrote stories, but

Portrait of author Marjorie Kinnan Rawlings, 1953. Courtesy of the State Library & Archives of Florida, Florida Memory.

they were such special tales that they opened a door for her readers into another world. America was expanding; cities were growing; and railroads, canals, and highways were being built. But this author brought her readers back to another time, when life was much simpler.

To write well, she had to know her subject well. She was able to tell what bird was flying overhead just by the way he flapped his wings. She could tell what season it was just by noticing what flowers were in bloom or what fruit was on the trees. She wrote in *Cross Creek*: "For the seasons at the Creek are marked, not by the calendar, but by fruits and flowers and birds."[2]

She immersed herself in learning all about the people around her. She had been a city girl. She had never known people like this. Why would people accept living so primitively in the backwoods all their lives?

She learned her subject well and then worked hard. Through her detailed writing, Marjorie Kinnan Rawlings made people both laugh and cry while reading her stories. A boy raising a pet deer and people living in a backwoods area came alive in her books. Someone speaking with Marjorie Harris Carr years later would describe the precious Ocklawaha River in these words: "This is the country made to glow in the writings of Marjorie Kinnan Rawlings."[3]

Soon after *The Yearling* won the Pulitzer Prize, a movie of her story was filmed in and around Ocala National Forest. Since that forest is now protected, many generations can not only read, but also see the wild woods described in "Miz Rawlins's" book. That whole country will "glow" for many years to come.

Marjorie Harris Carr worked along with her husband to save rivers and sea turtles and anything else that needed help surviving in a world that was being changed before it was understood.

Archie Carr saved sea turtle habitat by a pioneering experiment of tagging the turtles to see where they

Marjorie Harris Carr,
19??. Courtesy of the State
Library & Archives of Florida,
Florida Memory.

would naturally lay their eggs. His research saved miles of beaches in many countries that are now safe places for these fascinating creatures to have their young.

Archie and Marjorie Carr together worked to preserve parts of historic Paynes Prairie, to save Lake Alice on the University of Florida's campus, and to save old, moss-draped live oak trees in Micanopy. They worked together on turtle tagging and research and sometimes even published their findings together.

But Marjorie Carr's biggest job was stopping the cross-Florida canal. When she started that fight, she had no idea it would take such a major part of her life. Someone told her at the beginning that she'd still be at it in 20 years, and she told him he was crazy. Well, she was still fighting 40 years later! Even today, her children are still working to free that beautiful river.

Although it took longer than expected, it was worth the time.

By the time the canal project was halted in 1971, $73 million in taxpayer money had already been spent on it. Although now a greenway, the dam is still intact. But her distinguished leadership paved the way for many other successful environmental campaigns. Today, the Florida Defenders of the Environment's main purpose is still to restore and protect the Ocklawaha River. They also speak out on other related issues, such as managing growth in the state.

The three Marjories will not be forgotten. They have been awarded many honors. There have been high schools, government buildings, and visitor centers named after them. All three have been inducted into the Florida Women's Hall of Fame.

Each of these women was born in another state, but all three Marjories came to know and love Florida. So many changes happened during their lifetimes. When Ms. Douglas was born, women couldn't vote. When Ms. Carr wanted to attend college, few schools were open to women. She had the advantage of having married a professor at the University of Florida, so she could attend graduate school there. Soon those rules would change. Laws would change for women, and to better protect the environment.

Today, even with more protection for the environment, we must continue to be on our guard. Women and men alike need to be stewards, not destroyers, of our environment. Citizens, governments, and businesses need to work together for a world where we all can live in peace and harmony.

Marjory Stoneman Douglas wrote in her famous book, *The Everglades: River of Grass*, "The future for South Florida, as for all once-beautiful and despoiled areas of our country, lies in aroused and informed public opinion and citizen action. . . . We can still bring back much usefulness and beauty to a changed and recreated earth."[4]

Chapter 14

Florida's Future

Those of us who live in Florida today would probably not be here if it had not been for many projects that drained water off the rich land. The big problem was that those who blocked and rerouted pristine rivers did their work before they fully understood the consequences to the environment.

The state of Florida started out with an abundance of water. Rivers, lakes, creeks, streams—all still number in the thousands. Rainfall is usually abundant, and it is one of the wettest states in the nation. Its aquifers under the ground were formed millions of years ago. They are still full of clean, clear water. There are few places on earth that have such a valuable resource constantly available to its inhabitants.

But there are also few places on earth where the human population is growing so fast.

Winter visitors and year-round residents now use a tremendous amount of that fresh water every year. They use it not only for drinking, but also washing clothes and cars, flushing toilets, and sprinkling lawns. Population growth continues to be a challenge.

People love the warmth of the Florida sun, but they need to understand the fragility of the state. Cars, trucks, and buses are necessary, but people must understand that these vehicles create air and water pollution. Roads and railways are necessary, but care must be taken that they be built knowing and minimizing their effect on the environment and the ecosystems that surround them.

Farms, fertilizers, and mosquito control are necessary, but we must make sure they do more good than harm. When scientists during the Second World War created DDT, a very strong pesticide, it was used often in Florida to rid the state of mosquitos and other pests. It also harmed many birds and was toxic to humans. In 1962 Rachel Carson wrote a book called *Silent Spring*, in which she warned the public of the dangers of strong pesticides. Her voice was heard, and widespread spraying of pesticides has been controlled.

Legislation continues to be passed because of people willing to speak out. The federal Clean Water Act now requires each state to conduct water-quality assessments and to report their findings to the US Environmental Protection Agency.

We have a right to clean water and clean air. In 1981, the Save Our Rivers program was created. The Florida Forever program, which was the largest program in the country at the time for acquiring environmentally sensitive properties to protect them, was started in 2001.

The Everglades. Photo by Steve Sammons.

And there are other signs that changes are coming that will correct what was done without regard to the environment. Everglades National Park is still at the mercy of the engineers allowing water to flow into the park, but they are now hoping to relieve that problem by rebuilding parts of the Tamiami Trail.

Instead of the roadway remaining totally flat, now portions of the roadway are being raised to become bridges. Water can then flow freely under the bridges and it is hoped that some will flow naturally again into Everglades National Park. Wildlife, hopefully, will also return to those places.

Big Cypress has also been preserved, although the remains of an airport runway still scar the face of that wilderness. At least there are no supersonic booms to scare away the wildlife. Thank you, Marjory Stoneman Douglas and so many others.

Ocala National Forest has been preserved and Juniper Prairie Wilderness with its Yearling Trail is still a pathway for those who want to go back in time and imagine the days when the Crackers lived there. Thank you, Marjorie Kinnan Rawlings and so many others.

Visitors can also walk the trails along the Cross Florida Greenway and imagine the devastation that would have been if a cross-Florida canal had been built there instead. Someone said recently that the proposed canal was the single most dangerous threat to the water resources in the state in the twentieth century! A dam still stops the normal flow of the Ocklawaha, but at least the canal construction was stopped before it ruined any more ecosystems. Thank you, Marjorie Harris Carr and so many others.

At turtle nesting times, visitors can go to watch the turtles make their nests and deposit their eggs at protected areas of the seashore. The Archie Carr National Wildlife Refuge, managed as part of the Everglades Headwaters National Wildlife Refuge Complex, is just south of Cape Canaveral. The Complex includes the Pelican Island National Wildlife Refuge, the Archie Carr National Wildlife Refuge, and the Lake Wales Ridge National Wildlife Refuge. Thank you, Archie Carr and so many others.

Most of the people living in Florida today were born outside of the state. They may not know our history. One way to get to truly know the wonders on this peninsula is to get out into nature and discover the many wild places still left. A visit to any of the parks, preserves, or refuges can open one's eyes to the wonders around us.

"It is now abundantly evident that if our Paradise is to be protected, the initiative and force will have

to come from the grassroots. . . . It is the citizen who must lead; and to lead effectively the citizen needs to have certain basic knowledge."—Marjorie Harris Carr[1]

Afterword

Marjorie Kinnan Rawlings wrote at the end of *Cross Creek*:

I looked across my grove, hard fought for, hard maintained, and I thought of other residents there. There are other inhabitants who stir about with the same sense of possession as my own. A covey of quail has lived for as long as I have owned the place in a bramble thicket near the hammock. A pair of blue jays has raised its young, raucous-voiced and handsome, year after year in the hickory trees. The same pair of red-birds mates and nests in an orange tree behind my house and brings its progeny twice a year to the feed basket in the crepe myrtle in the front yard. The male sings with a *joie de vivre* no greater than my own, but in a voice lovelier than mine, and the female drops bits of corn into the mouths of her fledglings with as much assurance as though she paid the taxes. A black snake has lived under my bedroom as long as I have slept in it.[1]

She goes on to ask: "Who owns Cross Creek?" Cross Creek was her home for many years, where she had many exciting experiences and wrote many memorable stories. But who really owns any of the land on which we live? The earth belongs to all of us. And we, as tenants, must care for it and pass it on, in good condition, to future generations.

We can all follow in the three Marjories' footsteps. There are groups all over the state to join, and if we put our voices together, we will be heard.

Marjory Stoneman Douglas started the Friends of the Everglades in 1969, when she was almost eighty years old.

In 1994 a new group was started by fourth- and fifth-grade students at Howard Drive Elementary School in Miami, Florida, along with their teachers, Marta White-house and Connie Washburn. They called themselves the Young Friends of the Everglades, and they wrote the following mission statement: "To preserve and protect the Everglades, not just for us, but for future generations through education and children's awareness."

Young people are so important to spreading the word about the necessity for protecting the earth and our very lives. Florida's, and the world's, future depends on all of us.

We need more Marjories!

Who owns Cross Creek? The red-birds, I think, more than I. . . . Houses are individual and can be owned, like nests, and fought for. But what of the land? It seems to me that the earth may be borrowed but not bought. It may be used, but not owned. It gives itself in response to love and tending, offers its seasonal flowering and fruiting. But we are tenants and not possessors, lovers and not masters. Cross Creek belongs to the wind and the rain, to the sun and the seasons, to the cosmic secrecy of seed, and beyond all, to time.[2]

Chronology of The Three Marjories

1890, April 7, Minneapolis, Minnesota—Marjory Stoneman born.

1896, August 8, Washington, D.C.—Marjorie Kinnan born.

1915, March 26, Boston, Massachusetts—Marjorie Harris born.

1915—Marjory Stoneman Douglas moves to Florida.

1918—Marjorie Harris's family moves to Florida.

1927—President Calvin Coolidge signs the Rivers and Harbors Act, which authorizes surveys for a canal across Florida.

1928—Marjorie and Charles Rawlings move to Florida.

1935—President Franklin Delano Roosevelt authorizes funds for a ship canal across Florida.

1937—Marjorie Harris and Archie Carr marry near the Everglades.

1939—Marjorie Kinnan Rawlings wins the Pulitzer Prize for fiction for her book *The Yearling*.

1942—The US Congress authorizes the construction of a barge canal across Florida.

1942—Marjorie Kinnan Rawlings's book *Cross Creek* is published.

1946—*The Yearling* is made into a movie.

1947—Marjory Stoneman Douglas's book *The Everglades: River of Grass* is published.

1953, December 14—Marjorie Kinnan Rawlings Baskin dies at age 57.

1967—Marjory Stoneman Douglas's book *Florida: The Long Frontier* is published.

1968—Construction of the Rodman Dam on the Ocklawaha River is completed.

1969—Marjorie Harris Carr cofounds Florida Defenders of the Environment.

1971—Construction of the Cross Florida Barge Canal is halted.

1980—The Florida Department of Environmental Protection headquarters building in Tallahassee named for Marjory Stoneman Douglas.

1984—Marjorie Harris Carr awarded the Florida Audubon Society's Conservationist of the Year Award.

1986—The National Parks Conservation Association established the Marjory Stoneman Douglas Award to honor people who fight for the protection of national parks.

1987, May 21—Archie Carr dies in Micanopy at age 77.

1993—Marjory Stoneman Douglas is awarded the Presidential Medal of Freedom by President Bill Clinton for her collective work on environmental issues at age 103.

1997, October 10—Marjorie Harris Carr dies at age 82.

1998, May 14—Marjory Stoneman Douglas dies at age 108.

1998—Land for the barge canal is named the Marjorie Harris Carr Cross Florida Greenway.

2006—Marjorie Kinnan Rawlings Historic State Park is designated a National Historic Landmark.

Glossary

collaboration—working together

ecology—the study of the interactions between living things and their environment, which includes the idea that nature and wildness have value in our lives

ecosystem—the system whereby living things thrive (or not) in their environment

hydrologist—a scientist who studies the properties and circulation of water on earth and in the atmosphere

savanna—a flat plain, usually with rough grasses and scattered trees

sea turtles—reptiles that spend most of their lives at sea but depend on beaches for nesting sites. They can be found worldwide. Some types of turtles are green, loggerhead, olive ridley, and hawksbill.

supersonic—faster than the speed of sound

yearling—one that is a year old

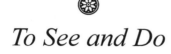

To See and Do

Parks and Historic Places

The Archie Carr National Wildlife Refuge

8385 South U.S. Highway A1A

Melbourne, FL 32951

321-723-3556

www.fws.gov/refuge/Archie_Carr

The Refuge stretches across more than twenty miles between Melbourne Beach and Wabasso Beach along Florida's east coast. It protects habitat for loggerhead and green sea turtles. Loggerheads have been designated a "threatened" species. Approximately 15,000–30,000 sea turtles nest there annually.

Sea turtle nesting season is from June to October. The best time to view sea turtles nesting is in June and July when guided, nighttime sea turtle watch programs are offered. The best time to see the hatchlings emerge from their nests is during turtle dig programs offered in August and early September. Call ahead to find out where and how to schedule a turtle walk.

Everglades National Park
40001 State Road 9336
Homestead, FL 33034
www.nps.gov/ever

The largest subtropical wilderness in the United States, the park protects 1.5 million acres in south Florida. Access by car is near the town of Homestead, the Royal Palm area, the Shark Valley entry near Miami, or the Gulf Coast entrance at Everglades City.

It is the third-largest national park in the lower forty-eight states, and it has been designated a World Heritage Site, International Biosphere Reserve, and a Wetland of International Importance.

The Marjorie Harris Carr Cross Florida Greenway
www.floridastateparks.org/trail/Cross-Florida
www.floridagreenwaysandtrails.org

Crossing central Florida from the Gulf of Mexico to the St. Johns River, the Greenway includes some historically significant areas, such as where the land was dug into for the Cross Florida Barge Canal.

Things to do along the Greenway: boating, horse/ equestrian trail, picnicking, canoeing and kayaking, birding, fishing, mountain biking, and walking.

Marjorie Kinnan Rawlings Historic State Park
18700 S. County Road 325
Cross Creek, FL 32640
352-466-3672
www.floridastateparks.org/marjoriekinnanrawlings

The Cross Creek home of Marjorie Kinnan Rawlings. The park rangers on site keep the home and yard looking like Marjorie just left. There are chickens in the yard and vegetables growing in the garden. A typewriter sits on a palm table on the porch. Guides share stories of "Miz Rawlins's" life.

Guided house tours and nature trails are available, and there is a picnic area in the adjacent county park.

The Rawlings Cracker house and property is a National Historic Landmark.

Marjory Stoneman Douglas Home
3744-3754 Stewart Avenue
Miami, FL 33133
www.historicpreservationmiami.com/douglas

Built for Marjory Stoneman Douglas in 1926, the English-style cottage was designated a National Historic Landmark in 2015. Marjory called it her "workshop," and lived here for seventy-two years, from 1926 to 1998. Shelves, tables, and even the floor held many, many books. Located in the Coconut Grove section of Miami. There are no public tours at the present time.

The Carr Cabin in the Ocala National Forest
www.carrfamilycabin.com/ocala-national-forest

Within the Ocala National Forest, this small cabin used by the Carr family was added to the National Register of Historic Places in 2017. The 300-square-foot cabin was built in 1938 and was used by three generations of the Carr family as a "getaway cabin in the woods." It is being restored by the Friends of the Carr Cabin, along with the Umatilla Historical Society.

Situated in deep woods, the cabin may be accessed only along private roads at this time. A nature trail will be blazed nearby so visitors may experience the deep woods. Tours of the cabin and the area have been given during Umatilla's Florida Wildlife Festival.

Juniper Prairie Wilderness in the Ocala National Forest
www.fs.usda.gov/recarea/ocala

The Ocala National Forest is between the Ocklawaha and St. Johns Rivers in central Florida. The Juniper Prairie Wilderness contains 14,283 acres and is very popular because of the Yearling Trail.

Paynes Prairie Preserve State Park
100 Savannah Blvd.
Micanopy, FL 32667
352-466-3397
www.floridastateparks.org/park/Paynes-Prairie

Ten miles south of the city of Gainesville, the preserve is just a portion of the prairie land that once covered this part of the state. William Bartram visited this open space in 1774 and called it the Great Alachua Savanna. Bartram described the prairie in detail in his book *Travels*, and when it was preserved, some of the same animals, including bison, were brought in to graze on the land. Plants native to the area were also replaced as much as possible. Today it is a diverse habitat for many creatures, including alligators, bison, horses, and nearly 300 species of birds.

Groups to Join to Help the Environment
Audubon Society
www.audubon.org
Check the website for your nearest chapter.

Florida Defenders of the Environment
www.fladefenders.org
P. O. Box 357086
Gainesville, FL 32635
352-475-1119

Friends of the Everglades
Young Friends of the Everglades
www.everglades.org
11767 S. Dixie Highway #232
Miami, FL 33156
305-669-0858

National Wildlife Federation
www.nwf.org
P. O. Box 1583
Merrifield, VA 22116
800-822-9919

The Wilderness Society
www.wilderness.org
1615 M Street NW
Washington, DC 20036
800-843-9453

Notes

Introduction

1. "in Wildness is the preservation" Henry David Thoreau, "Walking," in *Walden, Civil Disobedience and Other Writings*, ed. William Rossi (New York: W.W. Norton, 2008), p. 273.

Chapter 1

1. "the cleanest and purest of any river" Nelson Manfred Blake, *Land into Water—Water into Land: A History of Water Management in Florida* (Tallahassee: University Presses of Florida, 1980), p. 10.

2. "the greatest wonder I have ever seen" Gary Ross Mormino, *Land of Sunshine, State of Dreams: A Social History of Modern Florida* (Gainesville: University Press of Florida, 2005), p. 86.

Chapter 2

1. "Above us was the enormous Florida sky" Marjory Stoneman Douglas, *Voice of the River* (Sarasota, FL: Pineapple Press, 1987), p. 99.

2. "We could have been talking" Jack E. Davis, *Making Waves: Female Activists in Twentieth-Century Florida* (Gainesville: University Press of Florida, 2003), p. 152.

Chapter 3

1. "all readers concerned with" Jack E. Davis, *Paradise Lost? The Environmental History of Florida* (Gainesville: University Press of Florida, 2005), 307.

2. "Perhaps even in this last hour" Marjory Stoneman Douglas, *The Everglades: River of Grass* (Sarasota, FL: Pineapple Press, 2017).

Chapter 4
1. "In the summers, the sky would glow" Peggy Macdonald, *Marjorie Harris Carr: Defender of Florida's Environment* (Gainesville: University Press of Florida, 2014), p. 24.

2. "I was hooked with the idea" Michael Grunwald, *The Swamp: The Everglades, Florida, and the Politics of Paradise* (New York: Schuster Paperbacks, 2007), p. 204.

3. "The Everglades is a test" Ibid., p. 369.

Chapter 5
1. "'Me and her is buddies'" Marjorie Kinnan Rawlings, *Cross Creek* (New York: Simon & Schuster, 1942).

2. "He could open all the ice-box doors" Ibid., p. 163.

Chapter 6
1. "'The Creek!' he shouted" Marjorie Kinnan Rawlings, *The Yearling* (New York: Simon & Schuster, 1938).

2. "A spring as clear" Ibid., p. 4.

3. "Movement directly in front" Ibid., p. 204.

4. "My words was straight" Ibid., p. 73.

5. "The tree is beautiful" Marjorie Kinnan Rawlings, *Cross Creek* (New York: Simon & Schuster, 1942).

6. "Ponce de León discovered" Michael Gannon, *The New History of Florida* (Gainesville: University Press of Florida, 1996), p. 320.

Chapter 7
1. "We are bred of earth" Marjorie Kinnan Rawlings, *Cross Creek* (New York: Simon & Schuster, 1942).

Chapter 8
1. "it was the stupidity of killing everything" Frederick R. Davis, *The Man Who Saved Sea Turtles: Archie Carr and the Origins of Conservation Biology* (New York: Oxford University Press, 2007), p. vii.

2. "My aim was to become a zoologist" Ibid., p. 29.

3. "It was then that I became convinced" Peggy Macdonald, *Marjorie Harris Carr: Defender of Florida's Environment* (Gainesville: University Press of Florida, 2014), p. 31.

Chapter 9

1. "I just liked the look on their faces" Frederick R. Davis, *The Man Who Saved Sea Turtles: Archie Carr and the Origins of Conservation Biology* (New York: Oxford University Press, 2007), p. 2.
2. "world's greatest authority on turtles" Ibid., p. vii.
3. "Of his many collaborations" Ibid., p. 209.
4. " Those who dwell" Ibid., p. 263.

Chapter 10

1. "The first time I went up the Ocklawaha" Leslie Kemp Poole, interview with Marjorie Harris Carr, October 18, 1990.
2. "Once wilderness is gone" Ibid.

Chapter 11

1. "The salvation of the Florida scene" Ronald L. Myers and John J. Ewel, eds., *Ecosystems of Florida* (Orlando: University of Florida Press, 1990), p. xiii.

Chapter 12

1. "housewife from Micanopy" Peggy Macdonald, *Marjorie Harris Carr: Defender of Florida's Environment* (Gainesville: University Press of Florida, 2014), p. 8.
2. "make our peace with nature" Michael Grunwald, *The Swamp: The Everglades, Florida, and the Politics of Paradise* (New York: Simon & Schuster, 2007), p. 242.
3. "to prevent potentially serious environmental damage" Steven Noll and David Tegeder, *Ditch of Dreams: The Cross Florida Barge Canal and the Struggle for Florida's Future* (Gainesville: University Press of Florida, 2009), p. 266.
4. "I know you will not rest easy" Ibid., p. 300.
5. "I think elected officials listen" Macdonald, *Marjorie Harris Carr*, p. 194.
6. "one of the true pioneers of the movement" Noll and Tegeder, *Ditch of Dreams*, p. 324.

7. "Free the Ocklawaha River" Ibid., p. 325.

8. "The key to success" Jack E. Davis, *Making Waves: Female Activists in Twentieth Century Florida* (Gainesville: University Press of Florida, 2003), p. 185.

Chapter 13

1. "His fearful glance" Marjory Stoneman Douglas, *Freedom River: Florida 1845* (Coral Gables, FL: University of Miami, 1953), p. 4.

2. "For the seasons at the Creek" Marjorie Kinnan Rawlings, *Cross Creek* (New York: Simon & Schuster, 1942).

3. "This is the country made to glow" Steven Noll and David Tegeder, *Ditch of Dreams: The Cross Florida Barge Canal and the Struggle for Florida's Future* (Gainesville: University Press of Florida, 2009), p. 227.

4. "The future for South Florida" Marjory Stoneman Douglas, *The Everglades: River of Grass* (Sarasota, FL: Pineapple Press, 2017).

Chapter 14

1. "It is now abundantly evident" Peggy Macdonald, *Marjorie Harris Carr: Defender of Florida's Environment* (Gainesville: University Press of Florida, 2014), p. 122.

Afterword

1. "I looked across my grove" Marjorie Kinnan Rawlings, *Cross Creek* (New York: Simon & Schuster, 1942), p. 367.

2. "Who owns Cross Creek?" Ibid., p. 368.

Selected Bibliography

Bartram, William. *Travels*. New York: Literary Classics, 1996.

Douglas, Marjory Stoneman. *Alligator Crossing*. New York: John Day, 1959.

Douglas, Marjory Stoneman. *The Everglades: River of Grass*. New York: Rinehart, 1947.

Douglas, Marjory Stoneman. *Freedom River*. New York: Scribner's, 1953.

Lantz, Peggy Sias, and Wendy A. Hale. *The Wetlands of Florida: The Florida Water Story*. Sarasota, FL: Pineapple Press, 2014.

Macdonald, Peggy. *Marjorie Harris Carr: Defender of Florida's Environment*. Gainesville: University Press of Florida, 2014.

Rawlings, Marjorie Kinnan. *Cross Creek*. New York: Macmillan, 1942.

Rawlings, Marjorie Kinnan. *The Yearling*. New York: Scribner's, 1938.

Index

✺

About the Author

Sandra Wallus Sammons lived in Florida for thirty years, during which time she became an elementary school librarian in Mascotte, Florida, and learned of the need for biographies of famous Floridians for fourth- and eighth-grade students. She started writing and her books were published by Pineapple Press.

Photo by Steve Sammons.

She and her husband have spent the past seven years in the mountains of North Carolina, but upon returning to Florida and before a month went by, Sandy had a book in mind—again—that just "needed to be told."

Florida's history is so rich that she couldn't help sharing her enthusiasm for our fascinating state once again!